ILLUSTRATED BY JOHN BINDON

The Dinosaur Atlas

Don Lessem

KEY PORTER BOOKS

For Steven Spielberg,
who brought the wonder of dinosaurs to life for so many —DL

National Library of Canada Cataloguing in Publications Data
Lessem, Don
The dinosaur atlas: a complete look at the worlds of the dinosaurs/Don Lessem.
Includes index.
ISBN: 1-55263-540-6
1. Dinosaurs – Geographical distribution. I. Title.
QE861.5.L48 2003   567.9'09   C2002-905033-2

Key Porter Books Limited
70 The Esplanade, Toronto, Ontario Canada M5E 1R2
www.keyporter.com

Art Direction: Carol Moskot   Design: Vicki Hornsby
Printed and bound in Singapore
03 04 05 06 07 6 5 4 3 2 1

The publisher gratefully acknowledges the support of the Canada Council for the Arts and the Ontario Arts
Council for its publishing program. We acknowledge the financial support of the Government of Canada
through the Book Publishing Industry Development Program (BPIDP) for our publishing activities.

CONTENTS

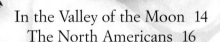

A Dinosaur Digger's World

THE SCIENTIST'S VIEW For the last 25 years, I've dug dinosaurs all over the world—and I've needed lots of maps to find my way to burial grounds in China, Mongolia, Argentina, the United States and Canada. Because the success of my work depends on good maps, I really appreciate atlases. But *The Dinosaur Atlas* is especially meaningful to me. An atlas is a wonderful way to illustrate the distribution and evolution of dinosaurs.

Dinosaurs changed both over time and in response to environmental changes worldwide. A true appreciation of dinosaurs is impossible without understanding how long and how widespread was their domain, and how many wonderful forms they took as land masses and sea levels changed. Thanks to my friend, author "Dino" Don Lessem, you can see all that right here—in *The Dinosaur Atlas*. I hope you find it as interesting as I have. And who knows? Maybe one day you'll be using it to help you hunt dinosaurs, too!

Dr. Phil Currie

CHIEF DINOSAUR PALEONTOLOGIST
ROYAL TYRRELL MUSEUM OF PALÆONTOLOGY
DRUMHELLER, ALBERTA, CANADA

DINO DON SAYS

DINOSAURS UP YOUR NOSE
Although dinosaurs were a big success—managing to rule the earth for 150 million years—they are only a short chapter in the history of life. If the Earth began at the bottom of your shoes, dinosaurs would appear somewhere up your nose and disappear at your forehead. If you think that's bad, try this: All of human life is just the split end of a hair on top of your head!

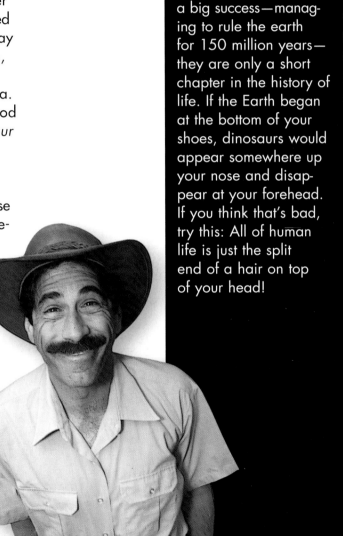

Dino Don's Dinosaur World

WELCOME TO THE WORLD OF DINOSAURS! Actually, *worlds* would be more accurate. Dinosaurs ruled the Earth for 150 million years, and during that time, the world changed from a single warm land mass into a series of continents that closely resemble the modern Earth. Despite these dramatic changes—changes that affected plant life, animal life and even the air—dinosaurs managed to thrive. How?

Dinosaurs were remarkable creatures—so remarkable that only a grown-up could fail to wonder at their greatness. As the world around them changed, the dinosaurs changed, too. Over millions of years, they evolved into bigger, stranger and more diverse creatures in order to adapt to their surroundings. This atlas is your guide to the amazing dinosaurs that walked, ate, fought and died in these long gone worlds. In the pages that follow, you'll learn how the world changed and how the dinosaurs changed with it. You'll learn about more than 50 types of dinosaurs—their names, food preferences, habits and enemies. You'll even learn how dinosaurs have helped paleontologists and other scientists understand more about the Earth's history.

So get going! Have a great trip, and watch out for dinosaurs!

"Dino" Don Lessem

HOW BIG WERE THE DINOS?
Use the boy and girl silhouettes throughout this book to see their sizes compared to you!

Wow!

The World Before Dinosaurs

THERE WASN'T ALWAYS LIFE ON EARTH. Five billion years ago, when the Earth was formed, not a single living thing walked the planet. Life began as a single cell—the kind that's only visible under a microscope—and took billions of years to develop into large animals.

We know that by about 600 million years ago, life had still not appeared on land. Although there were animals in the sea, they never grew larger than the size of your hand. It wasn't until about 300 million years ago that the first small amphibians walked ashore. Plants, insects and animals gradually began to conquer the land. As they did, the look of the Earth started to change.

About 250 million years ago, the Earth's Middle Age—or Mesozoic Age—began. This was the age of the dinosaurs, although it began without the dinosaurs themselves! In the early days of the Mesozoic, a period known as the Triassic, big reptiles called archosaurs (see below) ruled the land. Some, like the coffee-table sized aetosaurs were land-loving; others, like the seal-sized nothosaurs were water-dwelling. It was into this world that the dinosaurs first walked.

Saurosuchus

(SORE-oh-SOOK-us)

NAME MEANS "reptile crocodile"
GROUP Archosaurian reptiles

SIZE 20 feet (6 m) long **DIET** Meat
PLACE Worldwide

Archosaurs—the "ruling reptiles"—came in many odd shapes and sizes, including dinosaurs. Before dinosaurs, the most common archosaurs may have been the pig-like *rhynchosaur*, a small plant-eater with thick tusks that were probably used to dig for roots and other plants. Another reptile, *Saurosuchus*, was king of the pre-dinosaurian world. This killer crocodilian grew to lengths of more than 20 feet (6 m)!

Life before dinosaurs

3500 million years ago (mya)
first single celled animals:
blue-green algae

225 mya

300 mya

600 mya
flatworms

550 mya
trilobites
squid

500 mya
first vertebrates:
armored fish

400 mya
first animals evolve on land:
spiders, millipedes

375 mya *amphibians*

290 mya
reptiles

A Time for Dinosaurs

THE AGE OF DINOSAURS is broken down into three separate periods: the Triassic, the Jurassic and the Cretaceous. Three dinosaur periods, three dinosaur worlds. More than three worlds, in fact. During the dinosaur era, the land was constantly changing, just as it is today.

In the Triassic Period, more than 200 million years ago, the world was just a single continent, Pangaea, over the Equator. In the Jurassic, dinosaurs dominated life on land that had split into two supercontinents, Laurasia and Gondwana. These two great lands began drifting north and south, producing new groups of dinosaurs.

By the Cretaceous (145 million to 65 million years ago), the Earth's landmasses were taking on much the same shape as modern continents. Dinosaurs lived everywhere—from Australia, which was then in the Antarctic Circle, to northern Alaska, Mongolian deserts and parts of Alberta. Some Cretaceous dinosaurs even lived in polar lands, though there were no ice caps and few snowstorms in dinosaur days.

LATE TRIASSIC
220 million years ago

Lessemsaurus		
(LESS-em-SORE-us)		

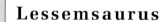

NAME MEANS "reptile named for 'Dino' Don Lessem"
GROUP Prosauropods

SIZE 30 feet (9 m) long
PLACE Argentina

DIET Plants

Lessemsaurus was a prosauropod—one of the giant plant-eating dinosaurs that appeared late in the Triassic. The biggest prosauropods, such as *Plateosaurus*, were nearly as long as a school bus, with heavy hind legs and lighter front limbs. They could stand on two legs or walk on all fours. These were the ancestors of the sauropods—giant plant-eaters like *Brachiosaurus* that became the largest animals ever to walk the Earth.

JURASSIC
160 million years ago

CRETACEOUS
100 million years ago

CALL ME A DINOSAUR Like volcanoes, mountains, continents and time periods, dinosaurs can be named for almost anything. Luckily, we're still finding dinosaurs so we get to name a lot. *Lessemsaurus* was found in Patagonia, Argentina, and named in 1999 for me. Why? Maybe because it had a small brain and a big belly—like me. At least it didn't have a mustache; dinosaurs didn't have hair!

The Changing World of Dinosaurs

THE LAND WASN'T THE ONLY THING changing during the dinosaur era. Landscapes and life forms underwent dramatic changes as well. When dinosaurs first appeared, the forests had no flowers—they were mostly made up of ferns, cycads (another spore-making plant) and conifer trees. During the Late Triassic, which was characterized by warm weather, the land was swept by monsoon rains. Thriving in these new conditions, mammals the size of mice appeared in the underbrush, and insects and lizards were everywhere.

In the Jurassic world seas divided the land into two supercontinents, resulting in more variations in climates and dinosaurs. Early in the Jurassic, deep lakes formed and dried along what is now eastern North America. Later, Europe was submerged. Birds appeared overhead and sharks multiplied in seas rich with heavily scaled fish. Ferns and horsetails lived in moist lands, while conifer trees inhabited drier areas.

The Cretaceous saw even more changes. As continents took shape, mammals grew to the size of cats, and flowers appeared on broadleaf trees. Huge flying reptiles called pterosaurs and many kinds of birds soared overhead. Giant turtles and huge lizards (mosasaurs) swam the oceans.

BIRD-HIPPED

LIZARD-HIPPED

DINOSAUR FLAVORS

The nearly 1,000 kinds of dinosaurs named are grouped in several ways. All dinosaurs are either ornithischians or saurischians. The ornithischians or "bird-hipped" dinosaurs were plant-eaters—from duckbills and horned dinosaurs to stegosaurs and armored dinosaurs. Saurischians or "lizard-hipped dinos" include all meat-eating dinosaurs or theropods, and the giant four-legged plant-eaters or sauropods and their ancestors, prosauropods. We now know that saurischians—not ornithischians—are the ancestors of birds.

LATE TRIASSIC
220 million years ago

JURASSIC
160 million years ago

CRETACEOUS
100 million years ago

11

The Late Triassic

WHERE DID THE FIRST DINOSAURS LIVE?

Anywhere they wanted, as the joke goes. In this case, though, it's true! In the Late Triassic period, all of the world's land was formed into a single mass along the Equator. The first dinosaurs roamed across this warm, rain-soaked continent.

We know what we know about the first dinosaurs thanks to fossil-rich rock from the Late Triassic. Dating back 228 million years, this rock is found primarily in Brazil and Argentina. It reveals the existence of meat-eating dinosaurs no bigger than poodles (see *Eoraptor* below). Within 20 million years, rocks from Europe, South Africa and the American Southwest show that meat-eaters and plant-eaters up to 20 feet (6 m) long had developed. What caused this tremendous increase in size? Scientists think that perhaps the dinosaurs' upright posture and superior speed gave them an edge over reptiles. Whatever the reason, dinosaurs were beginning to take over the land, growing in size and numbers.

By the end of the Triassic, dinosaurs dominated the reptile world; a world into which they had come less than 30 million years earlier. The age of dinosaurs had begun.

1	Eoraptor
	(Ee-oh-RAP-tore)

NAME MEANS "dawn thief"
GROUP Theropods

SIZE 3 feet (1 m) long   **DIET** Meat
PLACE Argentina

Eoraptor, which means "dawn thief," is named for its place at the dawn of dinosaur evolution. This small meat-eater, no bigger than a mid-sized dog, walked the land 228 million years ago. It was found in the mid-1990s in northwestern Argentina. The oldest nearly complete skeleton of a dinosaur, *Eoraptor* has features more primitive than both ornithischian and later saurischian dinosaurs.

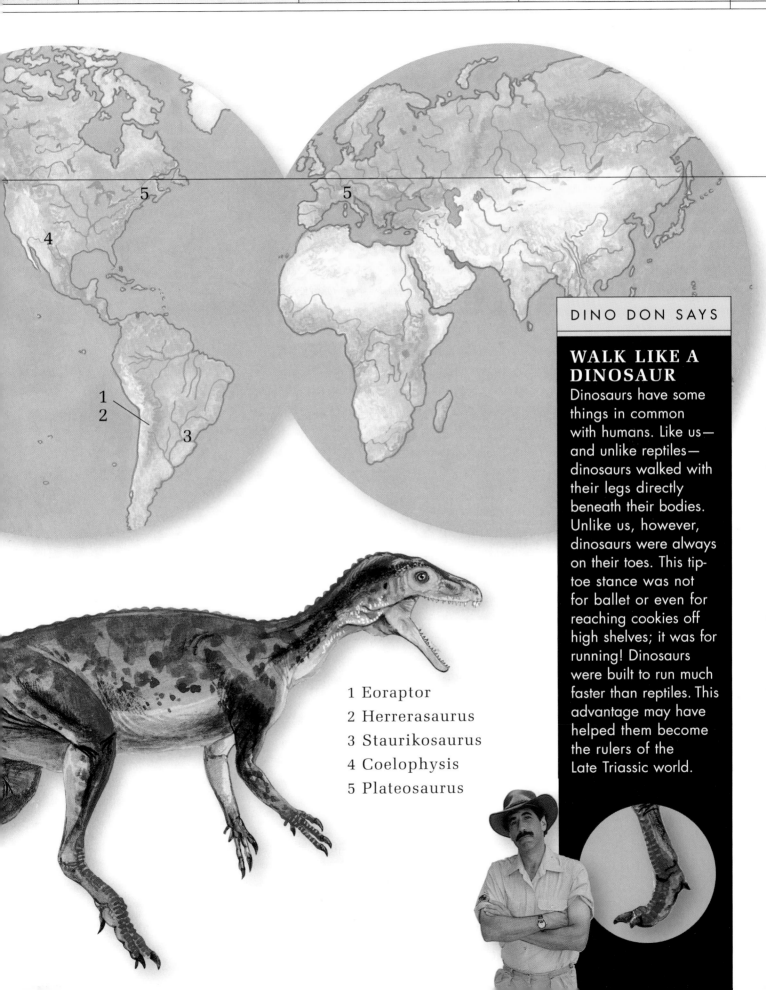

1 Eoraptor
2 Herrerasaurus
3 Staurikosaurus
4 Coelophysis
5 Plateosaurus

DINO DON SAYS

WALK LIKE A DINOSAUR

Dinosaurs have some things in common with humans. Like us— and unlike reptiles— dinosaurs walked with their legs directly beneath their bodies. Unlike us, however, dinosaurs were always on their toes. This tip-toe stance was not for ballet or even for reaching cookies off high shelves; it was for running! Dinosaurs were built to run much faster than reptiles. This advantage may have helped them become the rulers of the Late Triassic world.

In the Valley of the Moon

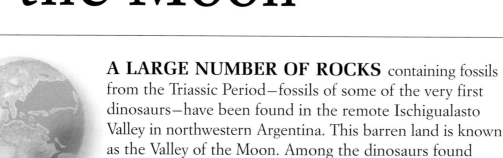

A LARGE NUMBER OF ROCKS containing fossils from the Triassic Period—fossils of some of the very first dinosaurs—have been found in the remote Ischigualasto Valley in northwestern Argentina. This barren land is known as the Valley of the Moon. Among the dinosaurs found there are the little *Eoraptor* (see page 12) and a much bigger meat-eater called *Herrerasaurus* (see below).

The first discoveries of the earliest dinosaurs, though, were made elsewhere in South America in the 1960s. In southern Brazil researchers uncovered parts of a small meat-eater that they named for the Southern Cross—a constellation visible in the skies over South America. It's name is *Staurikosaurus*.

2	Herrerasaurus
	(Her-rer-a-SORE-us)

NAME MEANS "reptile named for rancher Don Victorino Herrera"
GROUP Herrerasaurid theropods

SIZE 19 feet (6 m) long   **DIET** Meat
PLACE Argentina

Up to 19 feet (6 m) long, *Herrerasaurus* was a sharp-toothed killer with a flexible jaw that could swallow large chunks of meat. It had four fingers, instead of three or two, like later large meat-eating dinosaurs. The four-fingered hand shows that *Herrerasaurus* was among the more primitive dinosaurs.

14

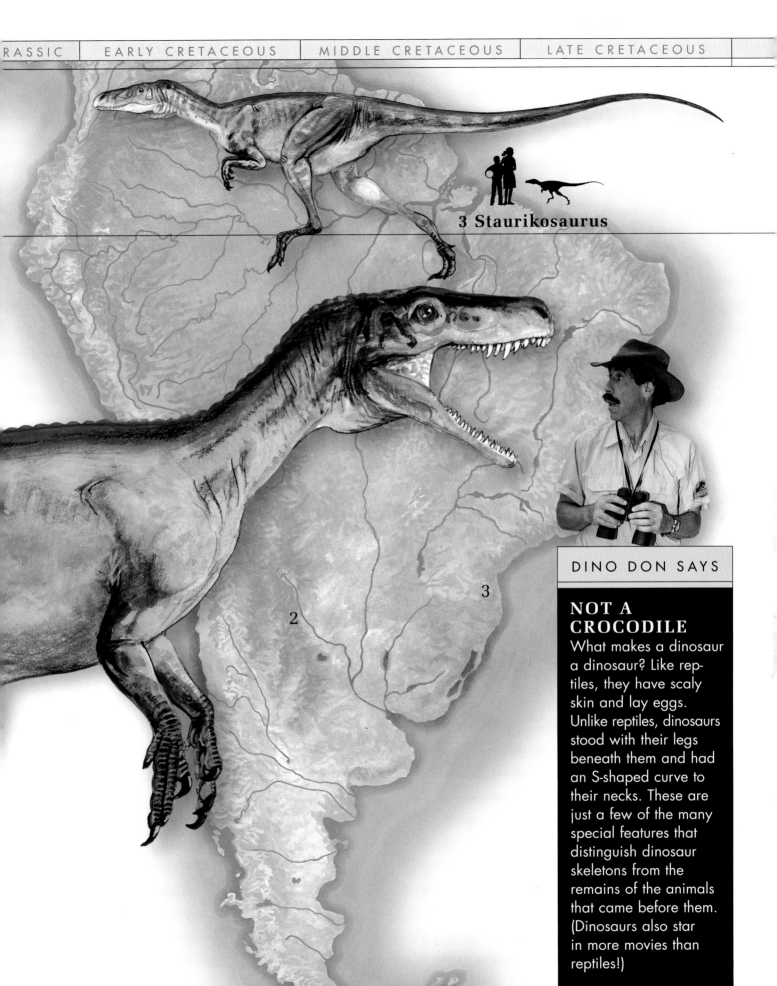

3 Staurikosaurus

DINO DON SAYS

NOT A CROCODILE

What makes a dinosaur a dinosaur? Like reptiles, they have scaly skin and lay eggs. Unlike reptiles, dinosaurs stood with their legs beneath them and had an S-shaped curve to their necks. These are just a few of the many special features that distinguish dinosaur skeletons from the remains of the animals that came before them. (Dinosaurs also star in more movies than reptiles!)

The North Americans

BY THE END OF THE TRIASSIC, dinosaurs ruled the earth. Larger, more primitive reptiles disappeared perhaps because dinosaurs were superior runners, hunters and feeders. Small, meat-eating dinosaurs like *Coelophysis* (see below right) appear to have lived and perhaps even hunted in large groups. Larger dinosaurs, both meat-eaters and plant-eaters, also appeared during this time.

Prosauropods such as *Plateosaurus* also roamed the land. Prosauropod footprints have been found along the east coast of North America along with those of mid-sized meat-eaters. Prosauropod bones have been found in modern-day China, South Africa, Europe, South America, Canada and the United States. These plant-eaters grew to over 20 feet (6 m) long.

A very different form of plant-eater, the bird-hipped (or ornithischian) dinosaurs are also found in Triassic rocks worldwide. The earliest of these chicken-sized dinosaurs were the fabrosaurids and hetero-dontosaurids. These were little plant-eaters with tiny teeth.

4

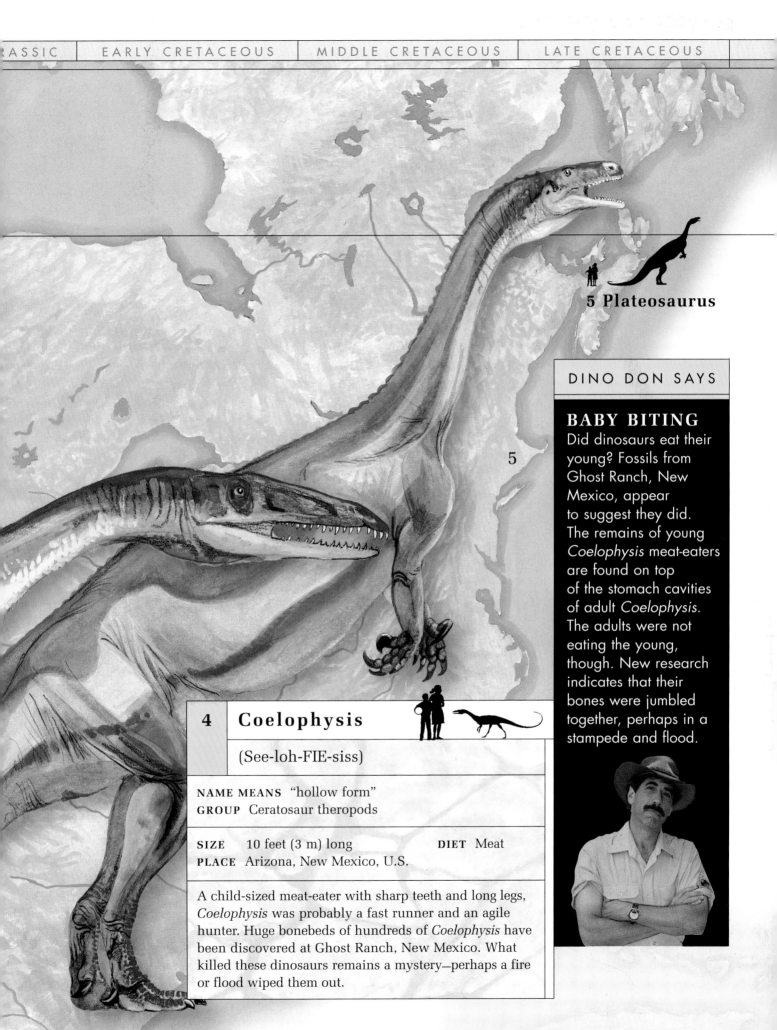

5 Plateosaurus

5

DINO DON SAYS

BABY BITING
Did dinosaurs eat their young? Fossils from Ghost Ranch, New Mexico, appear to suggest they did. The remains of young *Coelophysis* meat-eaters are found on top of the stomach cavities of adult *Coelophysis*. The adults were not eating the young, though. New research indicates that their bones were jumbled together, perhaps in a stampede and flood.

4 Coelophysis

(See-loh-FIE-siss)

NAME MEANS "hollow form"
GROUP Ceratosaur theropods

SIZE 10 feet (3 m) long   **DIET** Meat
PLACE Arizona, New Mexico, U.S.

A child-sized meat-eater with sharp teeth and long legs, *Coelophysis* was probably a fast runner and an agile hunter. Huge bonebeds of hundreds of *Coelophysis* have been discovered at Ghost Ranch, New Mexico. What killed these dinosaurs remains a mystery—perhaps a fire or flood wiped them out.

Jurassic Giants

Positions of continents, from Early through Mid to Late Jurassic

DURING THE JURASSIC PERIOD, one world became two when Pangaea divided. As the land on which they lived evolved, so did the dinosaurs.

Dilophosaurus (see below) gave way to larger and more heavily built meat-eaters. The stocky *Megalosaurus*, over 20 feet (6 m) long, has been found in many locations. By the end of the Jurassic, however, the massive *Allosaurus*, up to 35 feet (11 m) long, was king. This three-fingered killer had powerful arms and a body longer than a school bus.

Huge as they were, these meat-eaters were dwarfed by enormous plant-eaters. Sauropods grew to 130 feet (40 m) and five stories high—longer and taller than any other creatures before or since. Armored dinosaurs and plate-backed stegosaurs emerged from the "bird-hipped" line during this time. From the end of the Jurassic comes the first evidence of birds. *Archaeopteryx*, a weak flier from central Europe, appears to have descended from the meat-eaters.

6 Dilophosaurus

(DIE-low-fo-SORE-us)

NAME MEANS "two crested reptile"
GROUP Ceratosaur theropods

SIZE 23 feet (7 m) long **DIET** Meat
PLACE Arizona, Connecticut, U.S.; China

This 20-foot (6-m) long meat-eater gets its name from its double-crested head—which may have been designed to intimidate prey or attract mates. *Dilophosaurus* remains have been found in sites from Arizona to China. It appears to have been the top dinosaur hunter and scavenger of the Early Jurassic, since no meat-eater then grew as large.

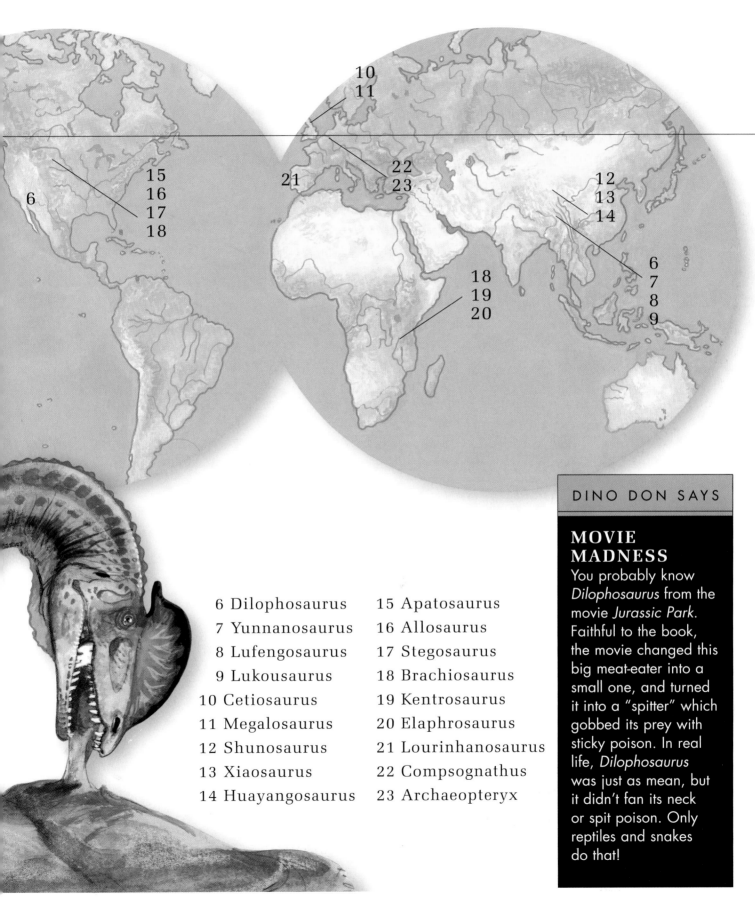

6 Dilophosaurus
7 Yunnanosaurus
8 Lufengosaurus
9 Lukousaurus
10 Cetiosaurus
11 Megalosaurus
12 Shunosaurus
13 Xiaosaurus
14 Huayangosaurus

15 Apatosaurus
16 Allosaurus
17 Stegosaurus
18 Brachiosaurus
19 Kentrosaurus
20 Elaphrosaurus
21 Lourinhanosaurus
22 Compsognathus
23 Archaeopteryx

DINO DON SAYS

MOVIE MADNESS

You probably know *Dilophosaurus* from the movie *Jurassic Park*. Faithful to the book, the movie changed this big meat-eater into a small one, and turned it into a "spitter" which gobbed its prey with sticky poison. In real life, *Dilophosaurus* was just as mean, but it didn't fan its neck or spit poison. Only reptiles and snakes do that!

China Clues

ALTHOUGH THE DINOSAURS ROAMED both Gondwana and Laurasia during the Jurassic, the best fossil evidence from this period has been found in modern-day China. These fossils suggest a land of seed plants and ferns populated by a few mammal-like reptiles, some rat-sized mammals and dinosaurs large and small.

From Yunnan province in southern China we know *Yunnanosaurus* (see below right) and *Lufengosaurus*, a prosauropod that bears a striking resemblance to the *Plateosaurus* found in Triassic Europe. *Lufengosaurus* was up to 20 feet (6 m) long and half as tall—a good height for reaching up into trees for food. *Lukousaurus* was a small meat-eater that probably fed upon little mammals and mammal-like reptiles.

Tatisaurus was another little dinosaur of a very different sort. It was an ornithischian plant-eater that chewed with small but powerful teeth. It also appears to have been an ancestor of the armored dinosaurs, or ankylosaurs. Armor was an important defense for many plant-eaters. Without large teeth or claws, they relied on their hard body covering to protect them from hunters. The later ankylosaurs, such as the Late Cretaceous Canadian dinosaur *Edmontonia*, had armor everywhere on their bodies, even on their eyelids!

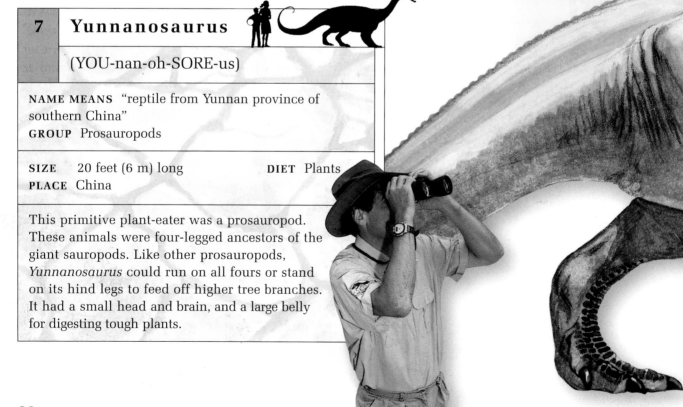

7	**Yunnanosaurus**

(YOU-nan-oh-SORE-us)

NAME MEANS "reptile from Yunnan province of southern China"
GROUP Prosauropods

SIZE 20 feet (6 m) long   **DIET** Plants
PLACE China

This primitive plant-eater was a prosauropod. These animals were four-legged ancestors of the giant sauropods. Like other prosauropods, *Yunnanosaurus* could run on all fours or stand on its hind legs to feed off higher tree branches. It had a small head and brain, and a large belly for digesting tough plants.

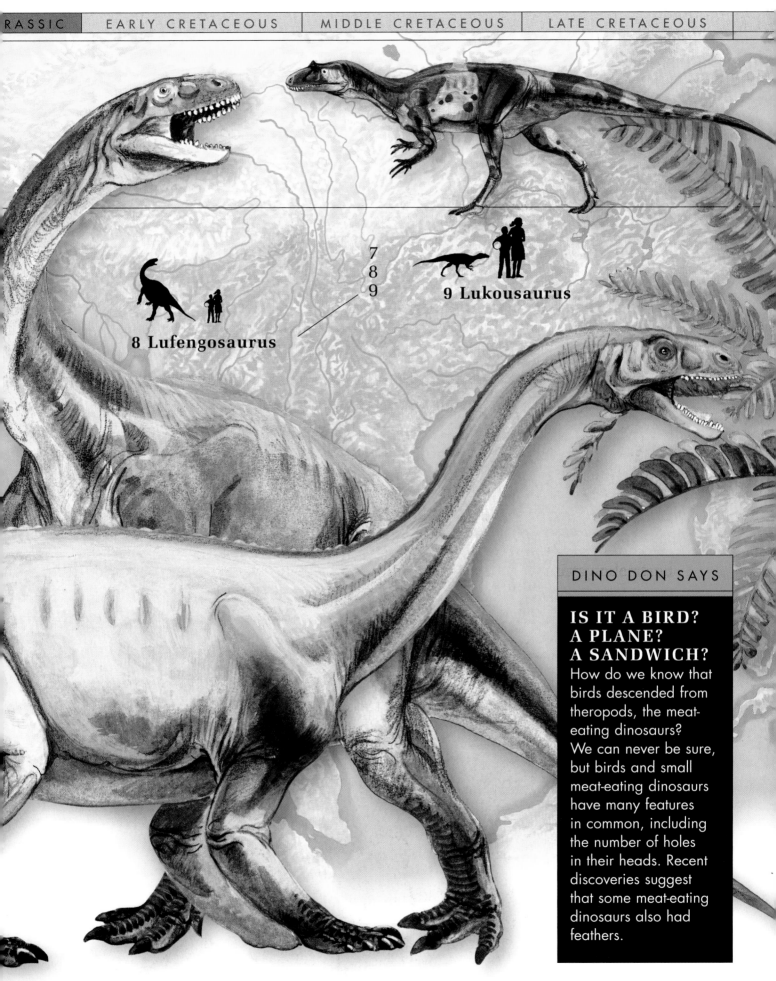

7
8
9

8 Lufengosaurus

9 Lukousaurus

DINO DON SAYS

IS IT A BIRD? A PLANE? A SANDWICH?

How do we know that birds descended from theropods, the meat-eating dinosaurs? We can never be sure, but birds and small meat-eating dinosaurs have many features in common, including the number of holes in their heads. Recent discoveries suggest that some meat-eating dinosaurs also had feathers.

21

Europe's Water World

WHILE DINOSAURS LIVED only on land, they had no trouble inhabiting watery territory. Nearly 200 million years ago, in the Early Jurassic, Europe was mostly underwater.

By the middle of Jurassic, sea levels had dropped and more European land was exposed. The supercontinent had fully divided into two separate land masses. Along with China, Europe provides the best evidence of dinosaur life 165 million years ago. *Megalosaurus* (a beefy meat-eater) and *Cetiosaurus* (a lumbering giant plant-eater, see below) are both known from England at this time. Both were discovered more than 150 years ago, making them two of the first dinosaurs ever identified.

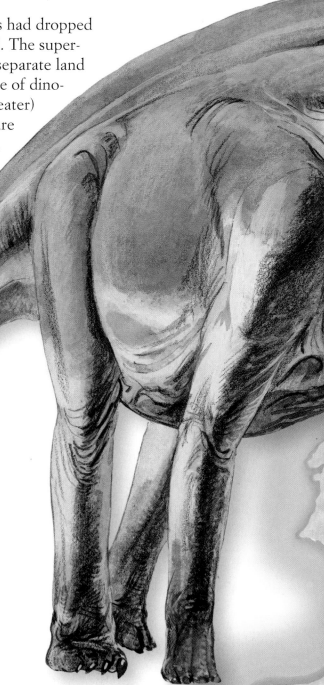

10	**Cetiosaurus**
	(SEE-tee-oh-SORE-uss)

NAME MEANS "whale lizard"	
GROUP Sauropods	
SIZE 50 feet (15 m) long	**DIET** Plants
PLACE England	

Cetiosaurus was named "whale lizard" for the shape of its backbones, which reminded scientist Sir Richard Owen of whale vertebrae. Owen is the man who invented the word "dinosaur" in 1841 for these "terrible lizards."

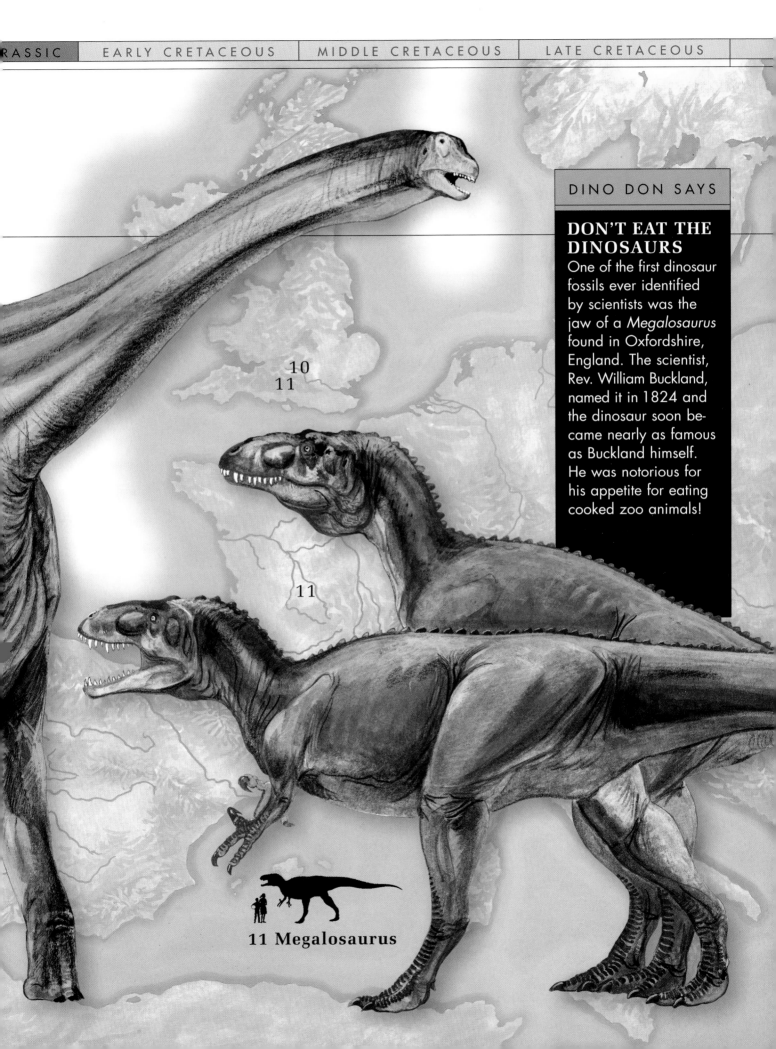

10
11

11

DON'T EAT THE DINOSAURS

One of the first dinosaur fossils ever identified by scientists was the jaw of a *Megalosaurus* found in Oxfordshire, England. The scientist, Rev. William Buckland, named it in 1824 and the dinosaur soon became nearly as famous as Buckland himself. He was notorious for his appetite for eating cooked zoo animals!

11 Megalosaurus

China's Graveyard

IN 1977, WHILE DIGGING for natural gas in south-central China's Dashanpu Quarry, workers made an amazing discovery. More than 100 complete dinosaur skeletons lay in the purple mudstone, perfectly preserved. All were dated to 165 million years old—the Middle Jurassic—a time not well known in the age of dinosaurs.

Three giant sauropods were found in the quarry, each more than 50 feet (15 m) long. *Shunosaurus* (see below right), *Datousaurus* and *Omeisaurus* were related to *Cetiosaurus* of England. The largest, *Omeisaurus*, had a hugely elongated neck and measured up to 68 feet long.

Smaller bird-hipped plant-eaters were also discovered: including the tiny *Xiaosaurus*, just 5 feet (1.5 m) long, and *Huayangosaurus*, an early 12-foot (3.5-m) plated dinosaur—or stegosaur—with spikes on its back instead of plates. The meat-eaters of Middle Jurassic China remain more mysterious. The largest, *Xuanhanosaurus*, was 20 feet (6 m) long, but has not been as well preserved as the wonderfully named *Gasosaurus*, a 13-foot (4-m) long killer.

14 Huayangosaurus

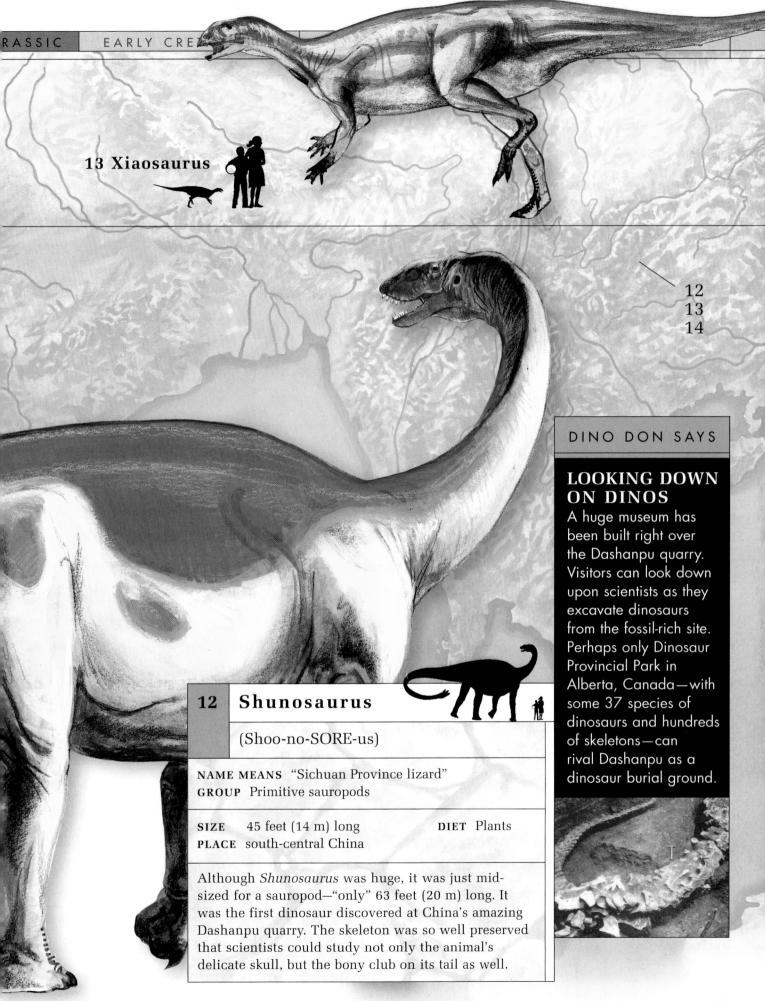

13 Xiaosaurus

12
13
14

LOOKING DOWN ON DINOS

A huge museum has been built right over the Dashanpu quarry. Visitors can look down upon scientists as they excavate dinosaurs from the fossil-rich site. Perhaps only Dinosaur Provincial Park in Alberta, Canada—with some 37 species of dinosaurs and hundreds of skeletons—can rival Dashanpu as a dinosaur burial ground.

12 Shunosaurus

(Shoo-no-SORE-us)

NAME MEANS "Sichuan Province lizard"
GROUP Primitive sauropods

SIZE 45 feet (14 m) long	**DIET** Plants
PLACE south-central China	

Although *Shunosaurus* was huge, it was just mid-sized for a sauropod—"only" 63 feet (20 m) long. It was the first dinosaur discovered at China's amazing Dashanpu quarry. The skeleton was so well preserved that scientists could study not only the animal's delicate skull, but the bony club on its tail as well.

The North American West

THE AMERICAN WEST was a forested land with shallow blue lakes 145 million years ago, and roaming this land were some of the biggest animals ever to shake the earth. The sauropod *Brachiosaurus* stood some six stories high. *Barosaurus*, *Diplodocus* and *Apatosaurus* (see below) also sauropods, reached 100 feet (30 m) including long whip tails that could snap a thunderous clap to frighten predators. *Seismosaurus* grew even larger, perhaps to 140 feet (42.5 m) long. *Stegosaurus*, the largest of all the plated dinosaurs, grew to the size of an ice-cream truck.

What did they all fear? *Allosaurus*. The largest of the Jurassic meat-eaters, *Allosaurus* had powerful arms and strong jaws and grew to 35 feet (11 m). It was capable of hunting down even the largest Jurassic sauropods.

Animals like many of these giants are known from the same time in Europe and East Africa. The similarity across continents suggests that these areas were not yet widely separated.

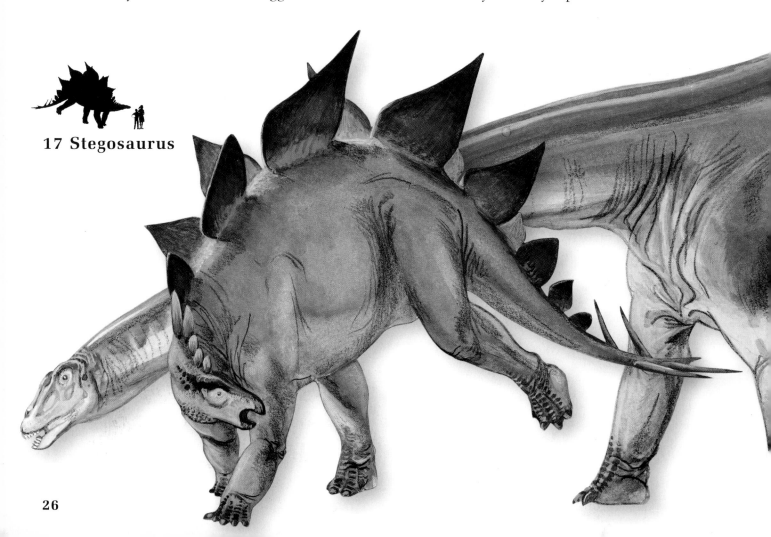

17 Stegosaurus

15 Apatosaurus

(a-PAT-oh-SORE-us)

NAME MEANS "deceptive lizard"
GROUP Diplodocid sauropods

SIZE 100 feet (30 m) long   **DIET** Plants
PLACE Oklahoma, Utah, Wyoming, Colorado, U.S.

Apatosaurus was the most misunderstood giant diplodocid—or whiptailed—dinosaur of Late Jurassic North America. Discovered in 1877 in Colorado, its remains were found again two years later in Wyoming. This time, however, the skeleton was wrongly named as a new animal: "Brontosaurus."

To make matters worse, another animal's skull found in the same quarry as *Apatosaurus* was mistakenly added to the "Brontosaurus" skeleton. It has taken a century to set the mistakes right.

DINO DON SAYS

CALL IT A DINOSAUR

The Great Bone Wars of the late 1800s in the American West led rivals Charles Othniel Marsh and Edward Drinker Cope to name more dinosaurs than anyone before or since. They also hid and bought bones, put heads on the wrong ends of skeletons, and incorrectly named dozens of animals, including "Brontosaurus."

16 Allosaurus

African Giants

NORTH AFRICA AND NORTH AMERICA were closely linked 145 million years ago. How do we know? Because the dinosaurs found on these two continents are so similar. And thanks to a massive expedition to East Africa nearly 100 years ago, we have the fossil evidence to prove it.

The most dramatic and best-known find from East Africa was *Brachiosaurus* (see below right). Also discovered were three other sauropods, more lightly built but still enormous. *Dicraeosaurus*, *Barosaurus* and *Tornieria* all browsed in this lush world, as did *Kentrosaurus*, a 15-foot (4.5-m) spiky stegosaur.

The hunters in this area included *Allosaurus*, the 20-foot (6 m) long *Ceratosaurus*, and a little *Elaphrosaurus* that might have may have preyed on the small ornithischian *Dryosaurus*.

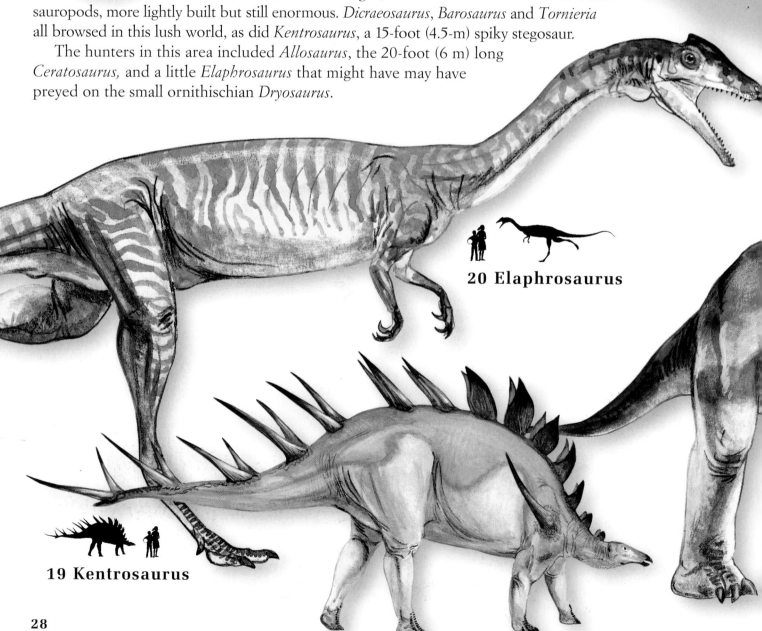

20 Elaphrosaurus

19 Kentrosaurus

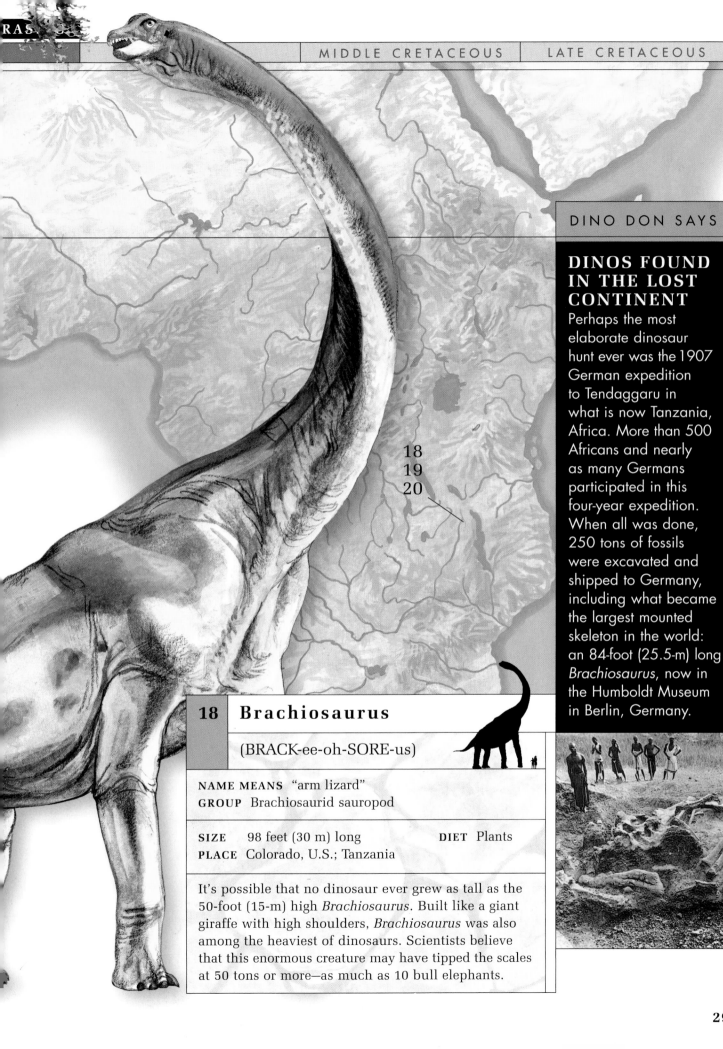

18
19
20

18 Brachiosaurus

(BRACK-ee-oh-SORE-us)

NAME MEANS "arm lizard"
GROUP Brachiosaurid sauropod

SIZE 98 feet (30 m) long **DIET** Plants
PLACE Colorado, U.S.; Tanzania

It's possible that no dinosaur ever grew as tall as the 50-foot (15-m) high *Brachiosaurus*. Built like a giant giraffe with high shoulders, *Brachiosaurus* was also among the heaviest of dinosaurs. Scientists believe that this enormous creature may have tipped the scales at 50 tons or more—as much as 10 bull elephants.

DINO DON SAYS

DINOS FOUND IN THE LOST CONTINENT

Perhaps the most elaborate dinosaur hunt ever was the 1907 German expedition to Tendaggaru in what is now Tanzania, Africa. More than 500 Africans and nearly as many Germans participated in this four-year expedition. When all was done, 250 tons of fossils were excavated and shipped to Germany, including what became the largest mounted skeleton in the world: an 84-foot (25.5-m) long *Brachiosaurus*, now in the Humboldt Museum in Berlin, Germany.

European Evidence

23 Archaeopteryx

WHAT KIND OF DINOSAURS roamed Europe 150 million years ago? Until recently scientists weren't sure. When we remember that much of Europe was underwater at the time, it's not surprising that seashore lagoons in what is now Germany have produced some beautiful fossils from the time. Although most of these animals were sea creatures, the oldest known bird, *Archaeopteryx*, and a small meat-eating dinosaur much like it, called *Compsognathus*, also fell into the lagoon and were preserved. Now, new discoveries in Portugal show that many of the dinosaurs known from Late Jurassic North America also lived in Europe at the same time. Brachiosaurs and allosaurs apparently lived on both continents and in Africa, too. This important fossil evidence suggests that these three continents were still linked.

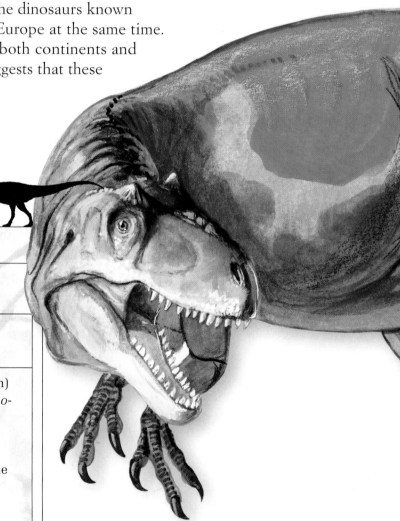

21	**Lourinhanosaurus**
	(Loh-REEN-yah-no-SORE-us)

NAME MEANS "Lourinha, Portugal, lizard"
GROUP Carnosaur theropod

SIZE 15 feet (5 m) long **DIET** Meat
PLACE Portugal

Lourinhanosaurus is a recently named, 15-foot (5-m) long meat-eater from Portugal. Although *Lourinhanosaurus* remains have not yet been found anywhere else, the shape of the Portuguese specimen's pelvis and hind limbs suggest that it was a relative of the allosaurs, which lived in North America at the same time. This dinosaur was found with smooth stones located nearby its stomach cavity, suggesting that it used the rocks to digest food.

22 23

22

21

DINO DON SAYS

EGGS IN THE POTTY A rare find of a *Lourinhanosaurus* (see left) embryo still inside its egg was made recently in Portugal. The discoverer was a two-year-old girl! Scientist Octavio Mateus's younger sister stopped near his dig site to go to the bathroom. When her mother looked down at her child's business, she saw bits of eggshell! The tiny embryo bones of *Lourinhanosaurus* were found nearby.

22 Compsognathus

31

The Cretaceous Period

Positions of continents, Early and Late Cretaceous

THE LAST DINOSAUR WORLD The world changed drastically in the Cretaceous—the last 80 million years of dinosaur life. Flowering trees spread through the forests. Mountains ranges like the Rockies, Andes and Himalayas were formed. India, a huge island then, swept north and crashed into Asia. Australia broke away from Antarctica, and Africa from South America.

Sea levels rose to record heights, and oceans covered much of Europe and the center of North America.

Birds spread through the air and flying reptiles reached 40 feet (13 m) in width. In the seas, huge reptiles grew as large as *T. rex*. On land, dinosaurs continued to take on many shapes and sizes (see *Microraptor* below). Then, relatively suddenly, they were gone (see pages 56–57)!

24	**Microraptor**
	(MY-crow-RAP-tore)

NAME MEANS "small thief"
GROUP Dromaeosaurid theropods

SIZE 22 inches (55 cm) long **DIET** Meat
PLACE China

This 2-foot (.65-m) long Early Cretaceous meat-eater from China is one of the most recently discovered dinosaurs. It's also the tiniest and most bird-like. Several feathered dinosaurs have recently been discovered in the Liaoning quarries of eastern China. The feathers of *Microraptor* are the most bird-like of any dinosaur feathers yet known. If, as scientists now think, birds are in fact dinosaurs, we cannot consider dinosaurs extinct.

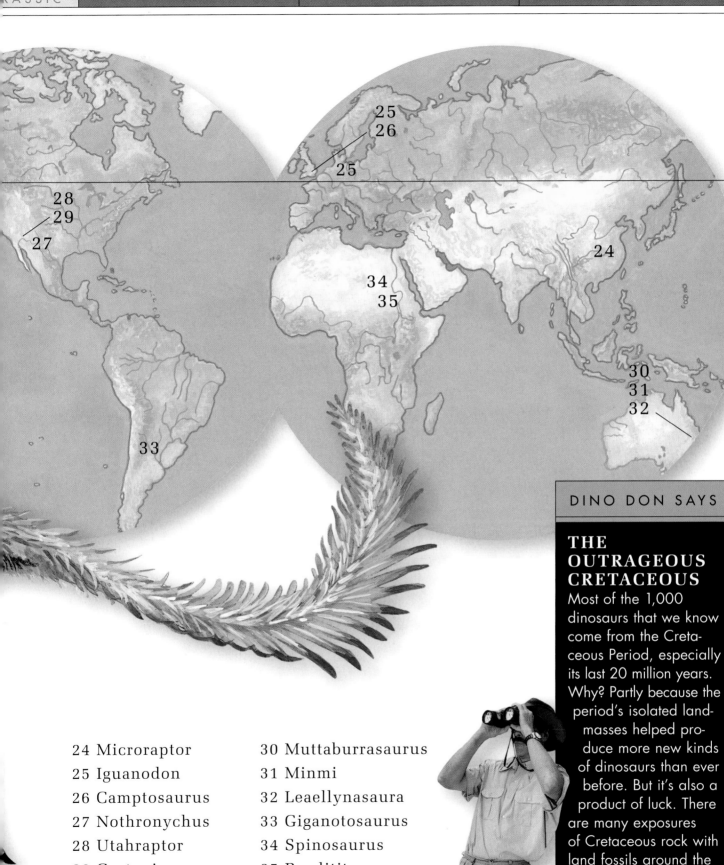

25
26
25

28
29
27

24

34
35

30
31
32

33

DINO DON SAYS

THE OUTRAGEOUS CRETACEOUS

Most of the 1,000 dinosaurs that we know come from the Cretaceous Period, especially its last 20 million years. Why? Partly because the period's isolated landmasses helped produce more new kinds of dinosaurs than ever before. But it's also a product of luck. There are many exposures of Cretaceous rock with land fossils around the world—far more than from other periods of dinosaur life.

24 Microraptor
25 Iguanodon
26 Camptosaurus
27 Nothronychus
28 Utahraptor
29 Gastonia

30 Muttaburrasaurus
31 Minmi
32 Leaellynasaura
33 Giganotosaurus
34 Spinosaurus
35 Paralititan

The Swamps of England

THUMBS AND TEETH Several new dinosaurs made their first appearance in the Early Cretaceous, while other familiar giants endured. Perhaps the most significant new development was the evolution of *Iguanodon* (see below). Iguanodontids were two-legged ornithischian plant-eaters some 20 feet (6 m) long. Although best known for its frightening thumb spike, *Iguanodon* prospered by developing a mouthful of hundreds of grinding teeth well-suited to the thick vegetation of swampy England and other habitats worldwide.

Another Early Cretaceous arrival was the "raptor" dinosaur, known to scientists as a dromaeosaurid. Raptors were predators with stiff tails and killer claws on each hand and foot. They are known only in the Northern Hemisphere, beginning in the Early Cretaceous with *Utahraptor*, nearly 20 feet (6 m) long. Their line ended in German shepherd-sized animals such as *Dromaeosaurus* which lived 50 million years later, near the end of dinosaur time.

Giant three-clawed meat-eaters—the end of the allosaur line of killers—reached record lengths in the Early Cretaceous. The biggest of all so far was *Giganotosaurus*, 42 feet (13 m) long, from Argentina.

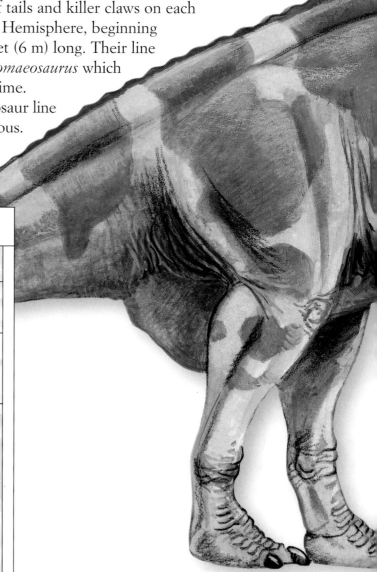

25	Iguanodon
	(Igg-WAH-no-don)

NAME MEANS "iguana tooth"
GROUP Iguanodontid ornithischians

SIZE 33 feet (10 m) long   **DIET** Plants
PLACE South Dakota, Utah, U.S.; Europe; Asia; North Africa

Iguanodon and its relatives are known from England, Belgium, other European sites, the United States, Asia, Africa and even Australia. Unlike their predecessors, these plant-eaters had long rows of teeth well-suited for grinding. Their descendants, the duckbilled dinosaurs, had hundreds of teeth. Not only could they chew with an up-and-down and back-and-forth motion, they could also grind side-to-side, as no other animal ever could.

25

26

25   25

25

THE DINO HIGHWAY

Millions of dinosaur tracks mark a north-south trail along what are now the Rocky Mountains of North America. What was going on? Dinosaurs were migrating in the Early Cretaceous. Ornithischian relatives of *Iguanodon*—like *Camptosaurus*—appear to have traveled in large herds in search of long summer grow-ing seasons to the north and warmer winter feeding grounds to the south.

26 Camptosaurus

Weird New Americans

A LONG-HIDDEN WORLD IS JUST NOW becoming known—the world in which the dinosaurs of western North America lived more than 120 million years ago. Many dinosaurs of the Early Cretaceous have only been discovered in the last decade. This was a time of transitions—the end of the allosaur and giant sauropod groups in the Northern Hemisphere, and the dawn of others, such as the iguanodontids and dromaeosaurids.

King of this domain was the 40-foot (12-m) long *Acrocanthrosaurus*, one of the last of the North American allosaur relatives. But another even deadlier dinosaur had recently appeared on the scene. *Utahraptor*, the first and largest of the known raptors, was a 20-foot (6-m) long hunter with a foot-long slashing claw on each limb. An *Iguanodon* relative, *Camptosaurus*, and smaller ornithischian dinosaurs such as *Dryosaurus* nibbled on plants. So did one of the largest of all armored dinosaurs, *Gastonia*, which had more armor than any other dinosaur.

Most mysterious of all is *Nothronychus* (see below), a dinosaur some 20 feet (6 m) long, named in 2001 from the Zuni Basin of northern Arizona. *Nothronychus* was a therizinosaur—one of a group of large sloth-like creatures with huge forelimbs that had previously been known only from later rocks in Asia.

DINO DON SAYS

GETTING SMALL Not all animals evolve into larger forms. Raptor dromaeosaurids, for instance, appear to start big with *Utahraptor* and become smaller over time, more commonly appearing as dog-sized dinosaurs such as *Velociraptor* in the Late Cretaceous.

27	**Nothronychus**
	(NO-thro-NYE-cuss)

NAME MEANS "sloth-like claw"
GROUP Therizinosaurid

SIZE 20 feet (6 m) long **DIET** Meat
PLACE New Mexico, U.S.

Nothronychus, like other therizinosaurs, was a descendant of the meat-eating dinosaurs. Its teeth, however, were shaped for chewing plants. The huge claws on these heavily built animals may have been suited for digging out roots or insects. We have no idea what it actually ate.

28 Utahraptor

28 29

27

29 Gastonia

Dinosaurs Down Under

DINOSAURS ON THE SOUTH POLE? Why not? For one thing, the pole was not as far south 110 million years ago as it is today. It was also warm enough to have no ice cap and only a dusting of snow. Midway through the Cretaceous, Antarctica had only recently separated from Australia and Africa, and the Australian continent still lay well within the Antarctic Circle—forcing its dinosaurs to live in darkness for part of each year!

A scattering of fossil finds suggest a rich dinosaur life. Just 100 miles (160 km) from the South Pole, researchers uncovered a 25-foot (8-m) long Jurassic meat-eater named *Cryolophosaurus*. Cretaceous armored dinosaurs are also known from Antarctica. On the southern coast of Australia, dynamiting has revealed the remains of hypsilophodontid plant-eaters no bigger than small kangaroos. The same site produced bits of what may be one of the fast, long-legged and toothless meat-eaters known as ostrich-mimics or ornithomimids. The best-known of the plant-eaters from the south coast is the child-sized hypsilophodontid *Leaellynasaura*. A small armored dinosaur named *Minmi* was found in Queensland as was a bumpy-snouted iguanodontid called *Muttaburrasaurus* (see below).

DINO DON SAYS

"DAD, I WANT A DINOSAUR!"

Leaellynasaura is one of the few dinosaurs to be given a female name. And a two-year-old was responsible. Paleontologists Pat and Tom Rich were asked by their then toddler, Leaellyn, to name a dinosaur after her. They did!

30 Muttaburrasaurus

(MUT-uh-BUR-uh-SORE-us)

NAME MEANS Named for town in central Queensland, Australia
GROUP Iguanodontidae

SIZE 24 feet (7 m) long **DIET** Plants
PLACE Australia

Muttaburrasaurus had a peculiar flat and bumpy snout. The bump in front of its eyes may have helped it call more loudly or sniff with more power. Its teeth were scissor-like and its thumb may have had a large spike. It may be related to the large North American plant-eater *Camptosaurus*.

30

31

32

31 Minmi

32 Leaellynasaura

Argentina and North Africa

DINOSAURS NEVER GREW BIGGER than they were 110 million years ago in the Southern Hemisphere. We know this thanks to some amazing recent discoveries.

In North Africa, an *Allosaurus* relative, *Carcharodontosaurus*, grew to nearly the size of *T. rex*—40 feet (13 m) long with a weight of seven tons. A new-found sauropod, *Paralititan*, stretched to twice as long as *T. rex* and may have weighed 80 tons!

Another North African giant was *Spinosaurus,* which had an unusual sail-shaped fin of bones along its back. Unfortunately, its dimensions remain a mystery: the best fossils of the animal were accidentally destroyed in a World War II bombing raid on Germany. Its contemporary, the *Iguanodon*-like plant-eater *Ouranosaurus*, also sported a sail-like back.

Even bigger animals grew in Argentina. *Giganotosaurus* (see below) is the largest meat-eater yet named—2 feet (0.6 m) longer and two tons heavier than *T. rex*. But even it lived in the long shadow of the largest animal ever to walk the Earth. The plant-eater *Argentinosaurus* stretched over 120 feet (36 m) long and weighed 100 tons. These and other South American dinosaurs show a very close resemblance to their North African cousins, suggesting that the two continents remained close to each other for longer than once thought.

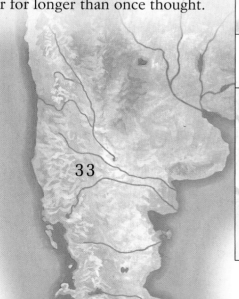

33

33	**Giganotosaurus** 
	(JIG-uh-no-toe-SORE-us)

NAME MEANS "giant reptile of the south"
GROUP Carcharodontosaurid theropod

SIZE 42 feet (13.5 m) long   **DIET** Meat
PLACE Argentina

The largest known meat-eater, *Giganotosaurus* had a skull 6 feet (2 m) long fixed with dagger-sharp teeth. It was a three-fingered animal, unlike the later, two-fingered *T. rex*. *Giganotosaurus* had a smaller brain, thinner teeth and a less powerful jaw than *T. rex*. And although *Giganotosaurus* was far more heavily built, *T. rex* was probably stronger, smarter and faster. What's the evidence? The size of *T. rex*'s braincase, its jaw bones and its longer legs.

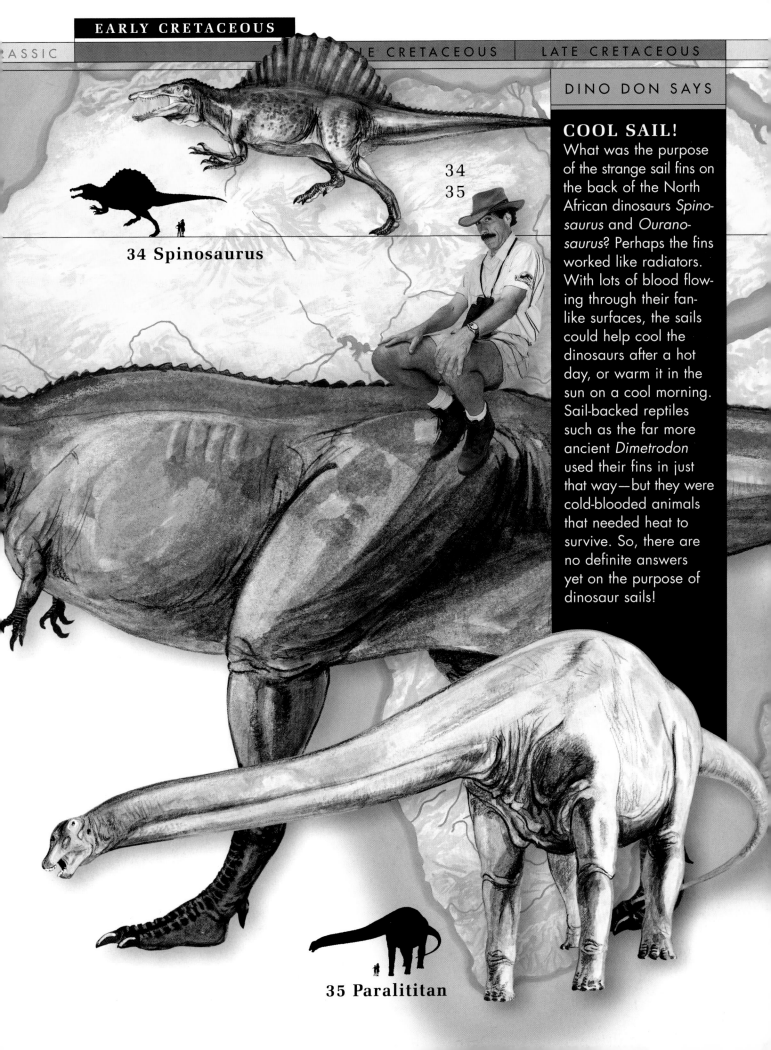

34 Spinosaurus

35 Paralititan

34
35

DINO DON SAYS

COOL SAIL!

What was the purpose of the strange sail fins on the back of the North African dinosaurs *Spinosaurus* and *Ouranosaurus*? Perhaps the fins worked like radiators. With lots of blood flowing through their fan-like surfaces, the sails could help cool the dinosaurs after a hot day, or warm it in the sun on a cool morning. Sail-backed reptiles such as the far more ancient *Dimetrodon* used their fins in just that way—but they were cold-blooded animals that needed heat to survive. So, there are no definite answers yet on the purpose of dinosaur sails!

The Late Cretaceous World

A GREAT FLOOD took place 100 million years ago, midway through the Cretaceous Period. But as the seas shrank in the Late Cretaceous, lands that had been separated were joined and dinosaurs began moving between continents again. A land link between North America and Asia allowed a new and terrifying group of hunters to move between the two continents. These were the tyrannosaurs, and *T. rex* was the last and nastiest of them all.

Duckbilled dinosaurs also developed during this time. Some, like *Lambeosaurus* (see below), had elaborate head crests, others did not. Raptors, armored dinosaurs, dome-headed pachycephalosaur plant-eaters and ostrich-mimic dinosaurs also moved freely between North American and Asia.

Giant sauropods like *Alamosaurus* came up from South America, while duckbills and armored dinosaurs moved nearly as far south as Antarctica.

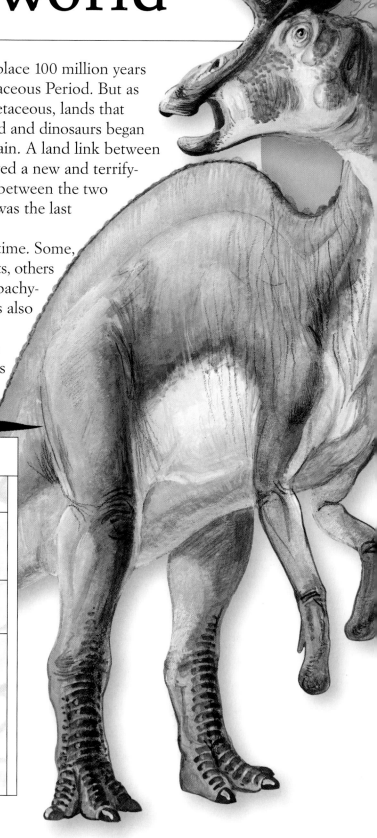

36	**Lambeosaurus**
	(LAM-bee-oh-SORE-us)

NAME MEANS "Lambe's lizard" for Lawrence Morris Lambe, a Canadian paleontologist
GROUP Hadrosaurids (duckbilled dinosaurs)

SIZE 30 feet (9 m) long   **DIET** Plants
PLACE Alberta, Canada; Montana, U.S.; Mexico

If you see a dinosaur with a fin-shaped crest on its head, there's a good chance that it is *Lambeosaurus*. The crest had hollow canals that connected to this "duckbill's" nostrils. Just as the body of a guitar makes the sound of the strings louder, the crest may have helped *Lambeosaurus*'s honks travel longer distances. Loud noises would have helped lambeosaurs traveling in large herds protect themselves from predators.

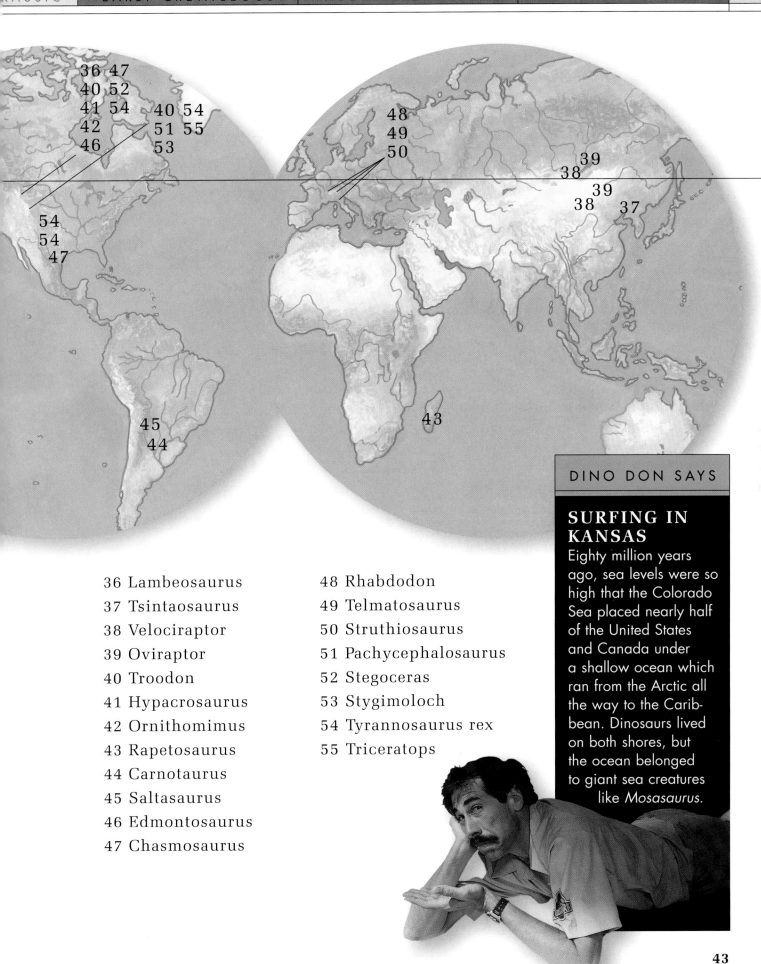

36 Lambeosaurus

37 Tsintaosaurus

38 Velociraptor

39 Oviraptor

40 Troodon

41 Hypacrosaurus

42 Ornithomimus

43 Rapetosaurus

44 Carnotaurus

45 Saltasaurus

46 Edmontosaurus

47 Chasmosaurus

48 Rhabdodon

49 Telmatosaurus

50 Struthiosaurus

51 Pachycephalosaurus

52 Stegoceras

53 Stygimoloch

54 Tyrannosaurus rex

55 Triceratops

DINO DON SAYS

SURFING IN KANSAS

Eighty million years ago, sea levels were so high that the Colorado Sea placed nearly half of the United States and Canada under a shallow ocean which ran from the Arctic all the way to the Caribbean. Dinosaurs lived on both shores, but the ocean belonged to giant sea creatures like *Mosasaurus*.

Going, Going Gobi!

ONE OF THE MOST historic and spectacular treasure grounds of dinosaur fossils is the Gobi Desert of Mongolia and China. Its fossil wealth was discovered in the 1920s by a real-life Indiana Jones. On expeditions for the American Museum of Natural History, Roy Chapman Andrews and his team discovered the first nest of dinosaur eggs ever known. Andrews' crew concluded the eggs belonged to *Protoceratops*, a small horned dinosaur common in the area. A toothless meat-eater discovered nearby was called *Oviraptor*, "the egg thief." They were wrong (see sidebar).

Since Andrews' time Russian, Polish and Chinese scientists, and western researchers have explored the Gobi Desert. They've discovered many animals closely related to those in North America—tyrannosaurs (*Tarbosaurus*), armored dinosaurs (*Pinacosaurus*), duckbills (*Tsintaosaurus*, see below), pachycephalosaurs (*Homocephale*), ornithomimids (*Garudimimus*), and "raptor" dromaeosaurids (*Velociraptor*), among others.

The Gobi treasures also revealed many beautiful skeletons of animals unlike those found in North America at the time. The horned dinosaurs are far smaller in Asia, while the long-armed therizinosaurs are only recently known from earlier times in North America.

37	**Tsintaosaurus**
	(TUH-sint-ow-SORE-us)

NAME MEANS Named for the region of northern China where it was found
GROUP Hadrosaur

SIZE 30 feet (9 m) long **DIET** Plants
PLACE northern China

This duckbilled dinosaur, or hadrosaur, has a bizarre head decoration. A spike sticks up from its forehead, like the unicorn of myth. Western scientists at first questioned whether the Chinese had placed this spike correctly, but now accept the positioning of this strange head crest.

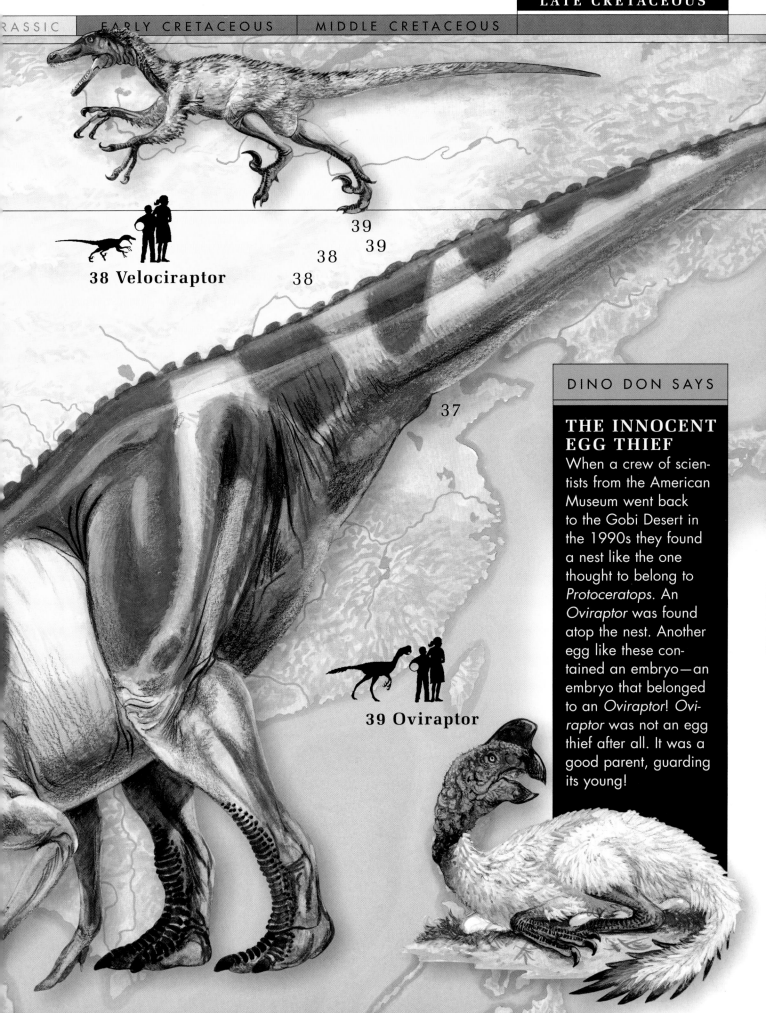

39

39

38

38

38 Velociraptor

37

39 Oviraptor

DINO DON SAYS

THE INNOCENT EGG THIEF

When a crew of scientists from the American Museum went back to the Gobi Desert in the 1990s they found a nest like the one thought to belong to *Protoceratops*. An *Oviraptor* was found atop the nest. Another egg like these contained an embryo—an embryo that belonged to an *Oviraptor*! *Oviraptor* was not an egg thief after all. It was a good parent, guarding its young!

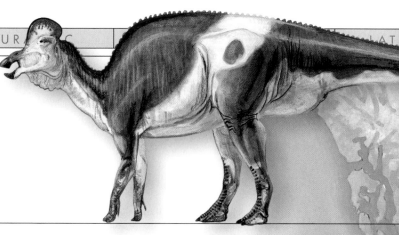

Canada's Badlands

THE WORLD'S GREATEST collection of dinosaur fossils is in the layered desert cliffs along the shores of the Red Deer River in Alberta, Canada, an area known as the badlands. So far, more dinosaur species and skeletons have been uncovered there than anywhere, and scientists are still digging!

Why did so many dinosaurs die here? Because so many lived here. In the Late Cretaceous, much of Alberta was a warm and fertile river delta, like Florida is today. When the rivers flooded, dinosaurs stampeded and sometimes drowned. Their bones were left behind, preserved in the sand and silt of the river bottom.

Among the many dinosaurs found in Alberta is *T. rex*'s smaller, earlier cousin, *Albertosaurus*. Ostrich-mimic toothless meat-eaters like *Ornithomimus* have also been found here—so well preserved that one can still see their horn-covered beaks. In the same region are many duckbill dinosaurs, such as *Hypacrosaurus*. Sometimes these are found with their eggs and embryos. Armored dinosaurs, with and without clubs, also browsed in western Canada. So, at the end of dinosaur time, did *T. rex*—a chunk of its poop was found in Saskatchewan!

40	Troodon
	(Tro-oh-DON)

| **NAME MEANS** "wound tooth" | |
| **GROUP** Troodontid theropods | |

| **SIZE** 6 feet (2 m) long | **DIET** Meat |
| **PLACE** Canada; China; Montana, U.S. | |

Troodon is another of the dinosaurs known from both Asia and North America. It doesn't look impressive. It's only as big as a 10-year-old, and very lightly built. But it has the largest brain compared to body size of any dinosaur or other animal of its time. With that mind, and keen eyes, agile fingers and speed, it was probably a very good hunter of small animals in the twilight hours.

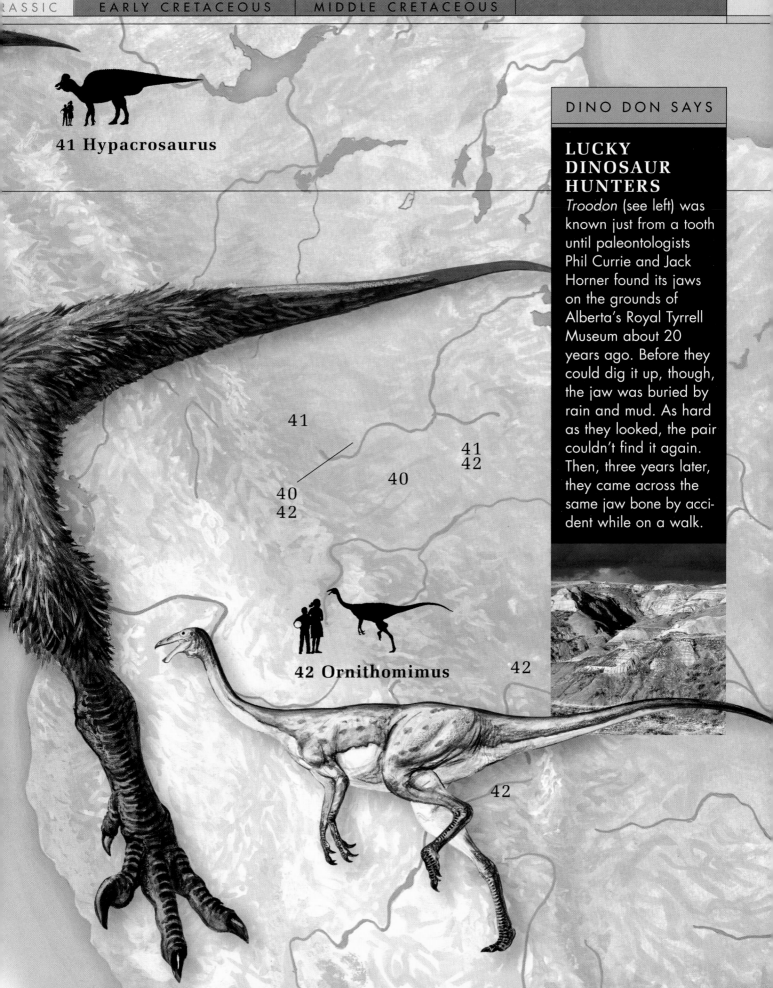

41 Hypacrosaurus

41

41
42

40

40
42

42 Ornithomimus

42

42

DINO DON SAYS

LUCKY DINOSAUR HUNTERS

Troodon (see left) was known just from a tooth until paleontologists Phil Currie and Jack Horner found its jaws on the grounds of Alberta's Royal Tyrrell Museum about 20 years ago. Before they could dig it up, though, the jaw was buried by rain and mud. As hard as they looked, the pair couldn't find it again. Then, three years later, they came across the same jaw bone by accident while on a walk.

Southern Giants

UNTIL THE END of the Late Cretaceous, the dinosaurs of South America had been isolated for many millions of years. Africa also was separated from other lands. These two continents had last been linked to each other 30 million years earlier.

Titanosaurs, the largest of the sauropod dinosaurs, dominated these lands. Huge as they were, their fragile heads were no bigger than a horse's. As a result, they are rarely preserved. Recently, however, a complete *Rapetosaurus* (see right) skeleton—including skull—was found in Madagascar. Titanosaur skulls have also been discovered in Argentina. It is in Argentina that we find the best fossil evidence for dinosaurs of this time. *Saltasaurus* was one of the last titanosaurs there: an armor-plated animal of 65 feet (20 m) or more.

And what did this giant plant-eater need protection from? *Carnotaurus*, perhaps. *Carnotaurus* was one of the strangest of all the abelisaurs—mid-sized meat-eaters with stubby faces and arms. *Carnotaurus*'s arms were even shorter than *T. rex*'s. It was still a menace to many plant-eaters, including the duckbills and armored dinosaurs that had ventured south-from North America.

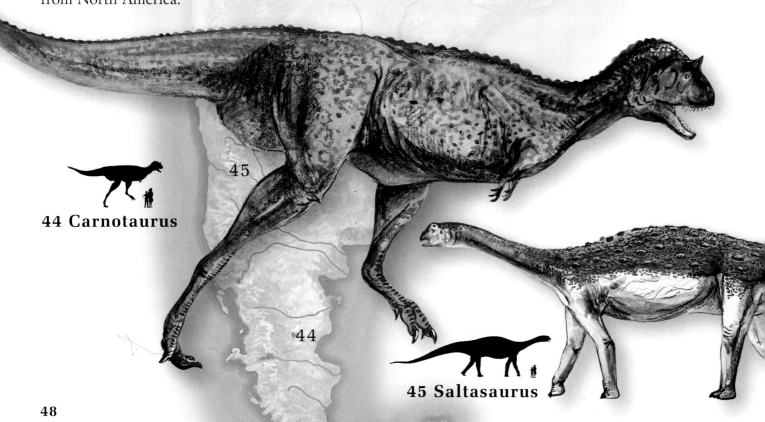

44 Carnotaurus

45

44

45 Saltasaurus

MOMMY DEAREST

When *Carnotaurus* was discovered, researchers at first overlooked the surrounding rock. When they returned to the site and looked more closely, they realized that the animal had been preserved with impressions of its skin—a dinosaur mummy! The *Carnotaurus* skin pattern was one of a regular series of bumps.

43 Rapetosaurus

(RAP-ee-toe-SORE-us)

NAME MEANS "Rapeto" lizard for mythical giant in Malagasy lore
GROUP Titanosaurid sauropods

SIZE 50 feet (15 m) long
PLACE Madagascar, Africa
DIET Plants

Rapetosaurus was a long-necked plant-eater from Madagascar. With a small head, long neck and long tail, it grew to 50 feet (15 m) long. Announced in 2001, it is one of the newest of all dinosaur names—taken from a trouble-making giant of local folklore on this African island.

43

Dinosaurs Can, Yukon, Too!

TODAY, THE HIGH ARCTIC IS SO COLD that the ground never thaws, and ice covers the land eight months or more a year. But 65 million years ago, Arctic temperatures rarely dropped below freezing, and the forested land looked much like woods near Seattle or Vancouver.

In the Late Cretaceous summer, long hours of daylight helped grow plants rich in nutrients. Fossil evidence suggests that dinosaurs sought out these plants. Some duckbills, like *Edmontosaurus* (see below), and horned dinosaurs such as *Chasmosaurus* may have migrated many hundreds of miles from their winter feeding territory in southern Alberta. Certainly, the remains of many of these dinosaurs—and tiny *Troodon* meat-eaters as well—have been dug from the cliffs along Arctic rivers in recent years.

46	**Edmontosaurus**
	(ED-mon-toe-SORE-us)

NAME MEANS "Edmonton reptile"
GROUP Hadrosaurid ornithopods

SIZE 40 feet (12 m) long   **DIET** Plants
PLACE Alberta, Saskatchewan, Canada; Montana, Wyoming, Colorado, Alaska, South Dakota, North Dakota, U.S.

Edmontosaurus is one of the largest and last of the duckbilled dinosaurs. It grew to 40 feet (12 m) long. Some duckbills had elaborate headcrests that may have been used to trumpet sounds. But *Edmontosaurus* belonged to a group of duckbills—the hadrosaurines—that had no crests. It is found in large numbers from Saskatchewan to Alberta, from Alaska to South Dakota. *Edmontosaurus* may have been one of the main menu items for a hungry *T. rex*.

47 Chasmosaurus

DINO DON SAYS

SNEEZING TOURISTS

Dinosaurs may have migrated to Alaska from Asia along with small mammals. If so, they could have brought diseases to their North America cousins—just as Europeans brought deadly flu germs to the Native Americans. It is a theory that makes sense but can never be proven.

46

47

46

46

46

Little Island Dinosaurs

A CENTURY AGO, A STRANGE nobleman from Transylvania began to study the dinosaurs found on his family estate. As Baron von Nopcsa expanded his search throughout central Europe, he found dinosaurs that were oddly short and primitive when compared to others from the Late Cretaceous. *Telmatosaurus* was the largest—a duckbill 15 feet (5 m) long. But at 500 pounds (225 kg), it was just one-tenth the weight and one-half the length of most duck-billed dinosaurs. Other finds include the tank-like small plant-eater *Rhabdodon* (see right), and the runty, armored *Struthiosaurus*.

Von Nopcsa had a theory for why these animals were so small. In the Late Cretaceous, Europe was a series of islands in a shallow sea, surrounded by volcanoes. In this stressful, isolated environment, dinosaurs might not have grown as large as elsewhere. Other smaller-than-average dinosaurs from the time have been found in France. Although scientists rejected Von Nopcsa's theories at the time, they are now widely accepted. Just as island animals today are often smaller than their mainland counterparts, the Central European dinosaurs of the Late Cretaceous were undersized.

49 Telmatosaurus

48 Rhabdodon

(RAB-do-don)

NAME MEANS "fluted tooth"
GROUP Iguanodontid ornithopods

SIZE 14 feet (4 m) long   **DIET** Plants
PLACE France; Romania; Austria; Hungary

Rhabdodon is known from France, Romania, Austria and Hungary. It appears to have been an iguanodon-type dinosaur, though small at just 14 feet (4 m) long. Iguanodontids had already disappeared in much of the world, but they may have survived in the isolation of Europe's islands.

48
49

48
49
50

DINO DON SAYS

THE MAD BARON

Baron von Nopcsa's theories may not have been accepted because he truly was crazy! He once wrote to the American president Theodore Roosevelt offering to lead a revolution in Albania and make himself king.

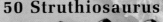

50 Struthiosaurus

In the Land of *T. rex*

IN EASTERN MONTANA, the world of the last dinosaurs is preserved as well as anywhere on Earth. The area is a dry badland now, but 65 million years ago, it was a thick forest of flowering trees and evergreens laced with rivers.

This was the kingdom of *T. rex*. In most communities, today and in dinosaur time, plant-eaters are by far the largest animals. But in Late Cretaceous Montana, *T. rex* was the biggest animal of all. *T. rex* had no rivals or threats on land.

T. rex had plenty of prey to choose from, as did the *Troodons*, dromaeosaur "raptors" and other smaller meat-eaters of the time. Crested and uncrested duckbills, armored dinosaurs with and without clubs, speedy ostrich-mimic dinosaurs and thick-skulled pachycephalosaurs (see below right) all roamed in *T. rex* country. Among the strangest looking plant-eaters were *Stygimoloch* and *Stegoceras*. Herds of horned dinosaurs such as *Triceratops* also called this region home. *Triceratops*, the largest of all horned dinosaurs, was 25 feet (7.5 m) long, but even its three long horns could not prevent *T. rex* from making it into a meal.

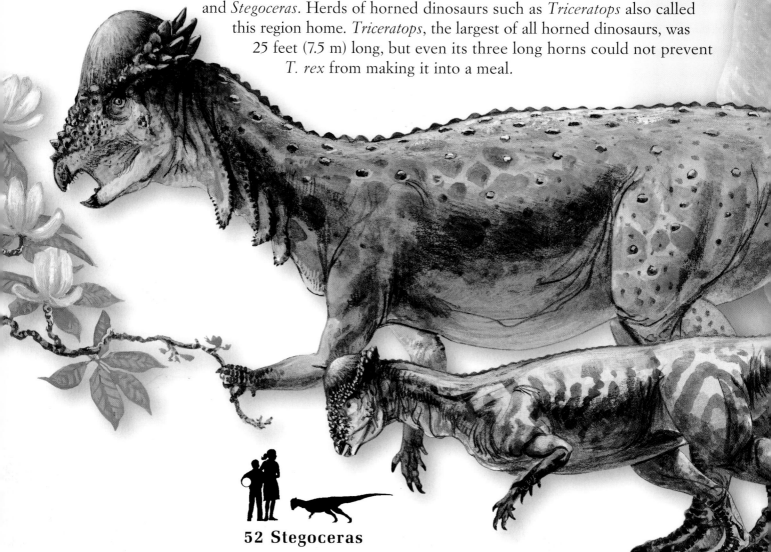

52 Stegoceras

51 Pachycephalosaurus

(PACK-ee-SEFF-oh-low-SORE-us)

NAME MEANS "thick-headed reptile"
GROUP Pachycephalosaurid ornithischians

SIZE 15 feet (5 m) long   **DIET** Plants
PLACE Alberta, Canada; Montana, Wyoming, South
Dakota, Alaska, U.S.

Pachycephalosaurus was one of the oddest plant-eating
dinosaurs. It had a thick skull—sometimes flat, other
times dome-shaped—that was often fixed with many
spikes. At 15 feet (5 m) long, it was the largest of the
"thick-headed" dinosaurs. Most pachycephalosaurs
such as *Stegoceras* and *Stygimoloch* were no bigger
than a third-grader.

51

52

51
52
53

51

DINO DON SAYS

**OFF YOUR
BUTT!** For many
years, scientists and
artists imagined that
the pachycephalosaurs
were head-butters. It
was thought that they
rammed each other
with their thick skulls in
contests for mates or ter-
ritories, like big horned
sheep do today. But
closer study has shown
that their rounded
heads would have just
slid off each other.
What's more, the
dinosaurs weren't built
for the shock of pound-
ing heads. These days,
scientists suppose that
pachycephalosaurs
used their thick heads
to whack each other
in the sides.

53 Stygimoloch

Good-bye, Dinosaurs!

FOR 163 MILLION YEARS, dinosaurs were a great success. Then, relatively suddenly, they were gone. What happened? Following the discovery of a huge crater off the coast of Mexico, the latest theory is that asteroids—rocks from space—crashed into the Earth. The force of this impact may have created waves of heat and water and clouds of dust which altered the world climate.

But this might have been just the nail in the coffin. It's possible that dinosaur life was already failing in kinds and numbers of animals. The climate of the Earth was gradually growing more extreme, and volcanic activity may have influenced the atmosphere, too. These are some of the latest ideas about why the dinosaurs died out. In truth, we just don't know—and we may never know—what wiped them out. We do know, however, that many other kinds of animals disappeared at the same time. Giant reptiles in the sea and air, and many forms of plants, did not survive the extinction event—whatever it may have been.

The good news is that the disappearance of the dinosaurs made more room for our ancestors—mammals. And dinosaurs aren't all extinct: their descendants live on in the sky. We call them birds.

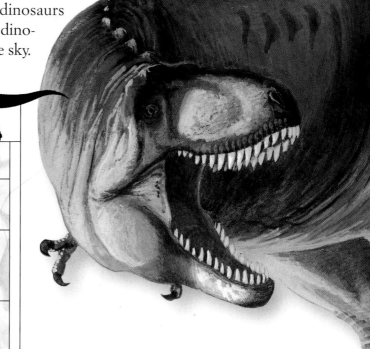

54	Tyrannosaurus rex
	(TIE-ran-oh-SORE-us rex)

NAME MEANS "tyrant lizard king"
GROUP Tyrannosaurid theropods

SIZE 40 feet (12 m) long   **DIET** Meat
PLACE Alberta, Saskatchewan, Canada; North Dakota, South Dakota, Montana, Colorado, New Mexico, U.S.

While *Tyrannosaurus rex* is no longer the largest meat-eater we know—that's *Giganotosaurus*—it remains the most powerful. With sharp, thick teeth the size of bananas, this massive creature could break through bone or saw off 500 pounds (225 kg) of meat in a single bite. But *T. rex*'s dinky arms were useless. Its two-fingered limbs were so short they could not even touch.

54

WHY GOOD-BYE?

Over the years, scientists have offered hundreds of theories for why the dinosaurs died out. Among them is the theory that the dinosaurs were either constipated or poisoned by new kinds of plants. Perhaps the strangest theory suggests that they polluted the air with their own gas! Today, cows are a leading source of methane gas in the atmosphere. Could lots of smelly dinosaur plant-eaters have choked the air? Unlikely. But gross!

55 Triceratops

Make Way for Mammals

NEAR THE END OF THE PALEOCENE EPOCH—several million years after dinosaurs—mammals the size of a rhinoceros appeared to feed on the new vegetation: grass. *Eobasileus* was one of the weirdest, with bony knobs and horns made of hair. Wolf-sized creatures like *Mesonyx* and cat-sized creodonts were among the meat-eaters of the day.

Mammals took to the sea and air as well. In the Eocene Epoch, 50 million years ago, bats appeared as did small whales like *Pakicetus*. The first horses—small woodland animals—also date from this time.

In the Oligene Epoch, 35 million years ago, the first dogs and cats evolved, as did huge horned browsers such as *Arsinotherium*. Biggest of all were the rhinoceroses (browsers with horns made of hair), including *Baluchitherium*, which reached up to 13 feet (4 m) at the shoulders!

The Miocene and Pliocene, up to 1.6 million years ago, saw the development of deer, giraffe and many kinds of elephants, including *Platybelodon*.

The Pleistocene Epoch lasted until just 10,000 years ago. In the last 2 million years, our own ancestors evolved. The first large-brained humans stood scarcely 4 feet (1.3 m) tall when fully grown, but they were nearly as brainy as us.

Our ancestors lived through the coldest years of an Ice Age that is still going on. A host of giant animals did not survive—dire wolves, sabre-toothed cats, giant ground sloths and woolly mammoths among them. What killed these great animals? Perhaps us. Or perhaps they died from diseases we brought with us as we traveled. While the answers aren't clear, one thing is certain: we would be very lucky to rule the changing planet for as long as the dinosaurs did—100 times longer than humans have been on Earth!

Platybelodon

Smilodon

Baluchitherium

Gastornis

(GAS-tor-niss)

NAME MEANS "Gaston's bird" and is named after the French physicist Gaston Planté
GROUP Gastornithidae

SIZE 7 feet (2.3 m) long **DIET** Meat
PLACE Ellesmere Island, Canada; New Jersey, New Mexico, Wyoming, U.S.; and Belgium, England and France.

The great killers that followed *T. rex* were not giant mammals but huge ground birds. More than 60 million years ago, *Gastornis*—once known as *Diatryma*—towered almost 9 feet (3 m) high. Its head was enormous and its massive beak could deliver crushing bites. Its long legs enabled it to run fast. With sharp talons on its feet, *Gastornis* could leap and slash at its prey.

DINO DON SAYS

UNDER THE SEA We think of dinosaurs as the most enormous animals that ever walked the Earth. That's true. But even bigger animals can be found in our oceans. The blue whale is almost 100 tons heavier than any dinosaur! Only the huge plant-eater *Argentinosaurus* can rival it for size. To put whale size in human terms, one blue whale weighs as much 4,000 ten-year-olds!

Learning More

The world is full of information about dinosaurs—from books and videos to museums and dig programs that you can participate in! Here are just a few places you can check out if you want to learn more.

COOL BOOKS

BARRETT, PAUL M., *National Geographic Dinosaurs*. National Geographic Society, 2001.

BENTON, MICHAEL, *The Encyclopedia of Awesome Dinosaurs*. Copper Beach Books, 2000.

DIXON, DOUGAL, *Dougal Dixon's Amazing Dinosaurs: The Fiercest, the Tallest, the Toughest, the Smallest*. Boyds Mills Press, Honesdale, Pennsylvania, 2000.

HALLS, KELLY MILNER, *Dino Trekking*. Wiley & Sons, 1996.

LAMBERT, DAVID, *The Ultimate Dinosaur Book*. Dorling Kindersley, New York, 1993.

LESSEM, DON, *Bigger than T. Rex*. Crown, New York, 1997.

LESSEM, DON, *Dinosaurs to Dodos: A Dictionary of Extinct Animals*. Scholastic, New York, 1999.

LESSEM, DON, *Dinosaur Worlds*. Boyds Mills Press, Honesdale, Pennsylvania, 1996.

LESSEM, DON, *Raptors*. Little Brown, Boston, 1996.

LESSEM, DON, *The Special Dinosaurs; Utahraptor, Seismosaurus, Ornithomimids, Troodon*. Lerner Publications, Minneapolis, 1995.

LESSEM, DON, *Supergiants*. Little Brown, Boston, 1997.

SVARNEY, THOMAS, AND PATRICIA BARNES SVARNEY, *The Handy Dinosaur Answer Book*. Visible Ink Press, Farmington Hills Michigan, 1999.

ZIMMERMAN, HOWARD, AND GEORGE OLSHEVSKY, *Dinosaurs: The Biggest, Baddest, Strangest, Fastest*. Atheneum, 2000.

COOL VIDEOS

BRITISH BROADCASTING CORPORATION, *Walking with Dinosaurs*, 2000.

DISCOVERY CHANNEL, *Bigger than T. Rex*, 1997.

DISCOVERY CHANNEL, *The Ultimate Guide to T. Rex*, 1997.

DISCOVERY CHANNEL, *When Dinosaurs Roamed North America*, 2001.

NOVA, *The Case of the Flying Dinosaur*, 1992.

NOVA, *Dinosaurs of the Gobi*, 1994.

NOVA, *The Hunt for China's Dinosaurs*, 1993.

NOVA, *T. Rex Exposed*, 1991.

COOL WEB SITES

www.DinosaurDon.com
"Dino" Don Lessem's official Web site includes a dinosaur dictionary, the latest dinosaur news, information on dinosaur digs and much more.

www.dinosaur.org/frontpage.html
The Dinosaur Interplanetary Gazette calls itself "the ultimate online dinosaur magazine." It includes a count of the current number of official dinosaurs discovered and has great dino pictures, too.

www.u.arizona.edu/~jmount/paleont.html
The University of Arizona's "Sci-Info" Paleontology & Fossil Resources site is a great starting point for finding out all kinds of information on dinosaurs. There are hundreds of links in over 30 categories, including "Evolution & Extinction," "Fossil Collecting" and "Researchers and Collectors: Personal Pages."

www.ucmp.berkeley.edu/diapsids/dinosaur.html
The Museum of Paleontology at the University of California, Berkeley, brings you "The Dinosauria" Web site—where you can find dinosaur facts and myths, information on early dinosaur discoveries in North America and great links to other dinosaur sites.

www.vertpaleo.org
Want to find out more about becoming a paleontologist? The Society of Vertebrate Paleontology Online has lots of information on paleontology as a job.

COOL DIG SITES
Many local science museums participate in single day and longer dig programs. Try your neighborhood science museum education department for more programs similar to those listed here.

Dinosaur Discovery Expeditions
Five-day trips with classroom, lab and dig components. Five-day dinosaur dig camp for families. Kids search for exact replicas of actual fossils. Professional paleontological leadership in a diversified, experienced program. *550 Jurassic Court, Fruita, CO 81521 Toll-free: 1-800-344-3466*

Dinosaur Expeditions, Museum of Western Colorado
Self-guided tours. Day digs available May through October on Thursdays and for groups of five or more almost anytime. *362 Main Street, Grand Junction, CO 81501 Tel: (970) 240-9210*

Earthwatch Institute
This worldwide non-profit organization offers volunteers an opportunity to assist scientists in fieldwork, including Montana dinosaur excavations. *Clock Tower Place, Maynard, MA 01754-0075 Toll-free 1-800-776-0188 www.earthwatch.org*

Museum of the Rockies Paleontology Field Program
An outstanding week-long program for kids and adults 10 and over, or kids 16 and over alone. Sleep in teepees. Work with paleontologists at famed Egg Mountain and Camptosaurus Quarry sites. *406 W. Kagy, Bozeman, MT 59717 Tel: (406) 994-6618*

Nomadic Expeditions
Mongolian Dinosaur Digs. Work with

renowned paleontologist Philip Currie in the Gobi Desert. *1095 Cranbury South River Road, Suite 20A, Jamesburg, NJ 08831 Toll-free: 1-800-998-6634*

Patagonia Tour
Seven days of sightseeing, digging and museum visits with paleontologists (Trelew, Neuquen, Buenos Aires, La Plata, Iguazu Falls). *Contact Dinosaur Productions, Tel: (617) 527-7796*

Royal Tyrrell Museum of Palaeontology
Work with museum staff in the world's best dinosaur dig sites. Weekend day digs May through August for ages 16 and up or ages 10 to 15 accompanied by an adult. Two-hour dig site tours in July and August. *P.O. Box 7500, Drumheller, Alberta Toll-free: 1-888-440-4240*

Wyoming Dinamation Digs
The digs are in June through August, with Como Bluff and Glenrock digs on alternate weeks.
• COMO BLUFF DIGS: Finding Allosaur, Apatosaur, Camarasaur, Megalosaur, etc. Dr. Robert T. Bakker and crew (Nancy Rufenacht, Melissa Connoly, Jordon Hand, and Russell Hawley) are the instructors.
• GLENROCK DIGS: Finding Triceratops, Torosaur, T. Rex, Edmontosaur, etc. Instructors are Sean Smith and Nancy Rufenacht with Dr. Bakker dropping in for a couple of days.
   The packages include three meals a day for five days while the dig is going on as well as dinner the night before and breakfast the morning after, motel room, local transportation, instruction (including lectures after dinner) and equipment. *Toll-free: 1-877-WYO-DINO E-mail: sjsmith@coffey.com*

Wyoming Dinosaur Center and Dig Sites
Mid-July to August are the most popular times, but it gets hot! Kid digs for children 8 to 13. *PO Box 868, Thermopolis, WY 82443 Toll-free: 1-800-455-3466*

COOL MUSEUMS

UNITED STATES
Academy of Natural Sciences
1900 Benjamin Franklin Pkwy.
Philadelphia, PA 19103
Tel: (215) 299-1000
www.acnatsci.org

American Museum of Natural History
Central Park West at 79th St.
New York, NY 10024-5192
Tel: (212) 769-5100
www.amnh.org

Carnegie Museum of Natural History
4400 Forbes Ave.
Pittsburgh, PA 15213
Tel: (412) 622-3131
www.carnegiemuseums.org/cmnh

College of Eastern Utah's Prehistoric Museum
155 E. Main St.
Price, UT 84501
Tel: (435) 613-5111
Toll-free: 1-800-817-9949
museum.ceu.edu

Dallas Museum of Natural History
3535 Grand Ave.
Dallas, TX 75226
Tel: (214) 421-DINO
www.dallasdino.org

Denver Museum of Nature and Science
2001 Colorado Blvd.
Denver, CO 80205
Tel: (303) 322-7009
Toll-free: 1-800-955-2250
www.dmns.org

Field Museum
1400 S. Lake Shore Dr.
Chicago, IL 60605-2496
Tel: (312) 922-9410
www.fmnh.org

Museum of Ancient Life
Thanksgiving Point
3003 North Thanksgiving Way
Lehi, UT 84043
Tel: (801) 768-2300
Toll-free: 1-888-672-6040
www.thanksgivingpoint.com/museum

Museum of Paleontology
University of California
1101 Valley Life Sciences Bldg.
Berkeley, CA 94720-4780
Tel: (510) 642-1821
www.ucmp.berkeley.edu

New Mexico Museum of Natural History and Science
1801 Mountain Rd. N.W.
Albuquerque, NM 87104
Tel: (505) 841-2800
museums.state.nm.us/nmmnh/nmmnh.html

Peabody Museum of Natural History
Yale University
P.O. Box 208118
170 Whitney Ave.
New Haven, CT 06520-8118
Tel: (203) 432-5050
www.peabody.yale.edu

Smithsonian Institution National Museum of Natural History
10th St. & Constitution Ave. N.W.
Washington, DC 20560
Tel: (202) 357-2700
www.mnh.si.edu

Wyoming Dinosaur Center
110 Carter Ranch Rd.
P.O. Box 868
Thermopolis, WY 82443
Tel: (307) 864-2997
Toll-free: 1-800-455-DINO
www.wyodino.org

CANADA
Canadian Museum of Nature
Victoria Memorial Museum Bldg.
240 McLeod St.
Ottawa, ON K1P 6P4
Tel: (613) 566-4700
Toll-free: 1-800-263-4433
www.nature.ca

Nova Scotia Museum of Natural History
1747 Summer St.
Halifax, NS B3H 3A6
Tel: (902) 424-7353
museum.gov.ns.ca/mnh

Royal Ontario Museum
100 Queen's Park
Toronto, ON M5S 2C6
Tel: (416) 586-5549
www.rom.on.ca

Royal Tyrrell Museum
Highway 838
Midland Provincial Park
Drumheller, AB T0J 0Y0
Tel: (403) 823-7707
Toll-free: 1-888-440-4240
www.tyrrellmuseum.com

AUSTRALIA
Museum Victoria
GPO Box 666E
Melbourne 3001, Victoria
www.museum.vic.gov.au

Queensland Museum
P.O. Box 3300
South Bank, South Brisbane
Queensland
www.qmuseum.qld.gov.au

AUSTRIA
Museum of Natural History
(Haus der Natur)
Museumsplatz 5
A-5020 Salzburg
www.hausdernatur.at/englisch.htm

Natural History Museum, Vienna
(Naturhistorisches Museum Wien)
Burgring 7
Vienna, 1014
www.nhm-wien.ac.at/d/
engvorschau.html

CHINA
Natural History Museum
126 Tianqiao Nan Jie
Beijing
www.bnhm.org.cn

**Palaeontological Museum
Zigong**
Beipei Museum
Dashanpu, Sichuan Province

DENMARK
Geological Museum
(Geologisk Museum)
University of Copenhagen
Oster Voldgade 5-7
DK-1350 Copenhagen K
www.nathimus.ku.dk/geomus/
welcome.htm

FRANCE
Museum of Natural History, Lyon
(Musee d'Histoire Naturelle
de Lyon)
28, boulevard des Belges
Lyon 69006
www.museum-lyon.org

**Museum of Natural History,
Paris**
(Musee d'Histoire Naturelle)
57 Rue Cuvier
Paris
www.mnhn.fr

GERMANY
**Hauff Museum of the
Prehistoric World**
(Urwelt-Museum Hauff)
Aichelberger Strasse 90
73271 Holzmaden
www.urweltmuseum.de

**Hessisches Landesmuseum
Darmstadt**
Friedensplatz 1
64283 Darmstadt
www.darmstadt.gmd.de/
Museum/HLMD

Jura-Museum
Jura-Museum Burgstr. 19
D-85072 Eichstätt
www.jura-museum.de

Museum fur Naturkunde
Zentralinstitut der Humboldt-
Universität zu Berlin
Invalidenstrasse 43
D-10115 Berlin
www.museum.hu-berlin.de

Museum Mensch und Natur
Schloss Nymphenburg
80638 Munich
www.musmn.de

Natural History Museum
(Staatliches Museum fur
Naturkunde)
Rosenstein 1
70191 Stuttgart-Nord
www.naturkundemuseum-bw.de

Paleontology Munich
(Paläontologisches Museum
München)
Richard-Wagner-Strasse 10
80333 Munich
141.84.51.10/palaeo_de/pmm/
PMM_Home.htm

**Senckenberg Natural History
Museum**
(Naturmuseum Senckenberg)
Senckenberganlage 25
D-60325 Frankfurt am Main
www.senckenberg.uni-frankfurt.
de/sme.htm

NETHERLANDS
**National Museum of Natural
History**
Darwinweg, Leiden
P.O. Box 9517
NL-2300 RA Leiden
www.naturalis.nl/asp/
page.asp?alias=naturalis.eng

Teylers Museum
Spaarne 16
011 CH Haarlem
www.teylersmuseum.nl/engels/
hal.html

SWITZERLAND
Naturhistorisches Museum
Augustinergasse 2
CH-4001 Basel
www.nmb.bs.ch

**Paleontological Institute
and Museum**
(Palaontologisches Institut
und Museum)
Karl Schmid-Strasse 4
8006 Zurich
www.palinst.unizh.ch

UNITED KINGDOM
City Museum & Art Gallery
Queen's Road
Bristol, BS8 1RL

Crystal Palace Park
Sydenham
London

Lyme Regis Philpot Museum
Lyme Regis
Dorset, DT7 3QA
www.lymeregismuseum.co.uk

Natural History Museum
Cromwell Road
London, SW7 5BD
www.nhm.ac.uk

**Sedgwick Museum
of Earth Sciences**
University of Cambridge
Downing Street
Cambridge
CB2 3EQ
www.sedgwickmuseum.org

Advanced Used to describe features that have evolved within a group as more specialized, or derived, than those of other members of its group. For instance, a two-fingered hand is an advanced feature in meat-eating dinosaurs. It evolved from the more primitive condition of three or more fingers.

Age of Dinosaurs Dinosaurs lived from the Late Triassic Period (228 million years ago) until the end of the Cretaceous Period (65 million years ago), a long time indeed for one life-form to exist.

Bird-hipped See Ornithischian.

Browse To feed on shoots, leaves and bark of shrubs and trees.

Carnivore A meat-eating animal.

Climate The average weather conditions in a particular part of the world. ("Weather" is the day-to-day variation in climate.)

Crest A descriptive term used here to mean the ridge or other projection found on the skulls of many dinosaurs, particularly the lambeosine hadrosaurs.

Cretaceous The third and last period of the Mesozoic Era and of dinosaur life, the Cretaceous Period lasted from 145 million to 65 million years ago.

Environment The living conditions of animals, including landscape, climate, plants and other animals.

Evolve To change over many generations to produce a new species, body feature or way of life.

Glossary

Scientists often describe the world of dinosaurs by using a hard-to-understand — and even harder to pronouce! — terms. If you're confused about what words like "Gondwana" and "Ornithischian" mean, consult this glossary!

Formation A geological term for the strata of rock deposited at a particular time and region.

Fossilized Turned into fossils.

Fossils Remains or traces of once-living plants or animals that are preserved, usually in rock.

Frill A descriptive term for the bony border or fringe of the dinosaur's skull, particularly the sometimes enormous, decorative fringe of bone on the horned, or ceratopsian, dinosaurs.

Gastrolith A stomach stone, in this case small rocks swallowed by many plant-eating dinosaurs to aid in digestion by grinding plants within the animal's gizzard. Some meat-eating dinosaurs had gastroliths, perhaps to aid in balance while swimming.

Gondwana The more southern of the two supercontinents formed by the breakup of Pangaea in the Age of Dinosaurs, including land that is now Australia, South America, Africa, Antarctica, Madagascar and India.

Habitat The local area in which an animal or plant lives, for example, a desert, forest or lake.

Herbivore A plant-eating animal.

Horn A pointed structure that may be made of bone or hair.

Impression A mark or print in the surface of the ground or a rock made by something pressing against or in it.

Jurassic The second period of the Mesozoic Era and of dinosaur life, the Jurassic Period lasted from 200 million to 145 million years ago.

Laurasia The more northern of the two supercontinents formed by the breakup of Pangaea around 200 million years ago. Laurasia is made up of what is now North America, Europe and most of Asia.

Lizard-hipped *See* Saurischian.

Mammals An order of animals with hair, whose members nurse their babies. Mammals were present throughout the Cretaceous Period, though they never grew larger than housecats.

Mesozoic One of the major eras of earth's history, from 245 million to 65 million years ago. It was the time when dinosaurs, flying reptiles, and many other life forms lived, and when mammals and birds first evolved.

Migrate To move from place to place as conditions change or for mating or reproduction.

Ornithischian One of the two orders of dinosaurs, based by traditional analysis on hip anatomy. These are bird-hipped dinosaurs that, like birds, have a pubic bone that lies parallel to another hip-bone, the ischium. Stegosaurs and armored, dome-headed and duckbilled dinosaurs are ornithischian. All ornithischians are plant-eaters.

Paleontologist A scientist who studies fossils of plant and animal life of the past.

Pangaea The name given to the supercontinent that existed in the Triassic Period, approximately 230 million years ago, when all the land masses of the earth were joined.

Plate A smooth, flat, bony piece that formed part of an armored covering on many dinosaurs, including all ankylosaurs and some titanosaurid sauropods.

Primitive This term is used to describe dinosaur features that are simple, or conservative. For instance, among dinosaurs, a five-toed foot is a primitive condition. Individual kinds of dinosaurs within a group will lose many of their primitive features over millions of years. But sometimes certain primitive features are retained by individual kinds of dinosaurs.

Reptiles Cold-blooded vertebrate animals with scales and without hair or feathers or a fully upright gait that reproduce by laying hard-shelled or leathery eggs on land. Snakes, lizards, turtles and crocodiles are some modern types of reptiles.

Saurischian The second order of dinosaurs based on hip anatomy. These lizard-hipped dinosaurs had a long pubis pointing forward and down from the hip socket. The meat-eating theropods and the giant herbivore sauropods are saurischians.

Sauropod Large plant-eating saurischian dinosaurs. This group included the largest dinosaurs known, some of which were more than 100 feet (30 m) long.

Scavenger A meat-eating animal that eats the bodies of animals already dead.

Scutes Armor plates found on many plant-eating dinosaurs.

Spine A bony, pointed projection, often used here interchangeably with "spike," which refers to the large, tapering bone outgrowths on many armored and plate-backed dinosaurs.

Tail club A large knob of bone at the tip of the tail vertebrae that was present on ankylosaurid armored dinosaurs and some sauropod dinosaurs.

Theropods Two-legged, meat-eating, "lizard-hipped" dinosaurs ranging in size from tiny hunters smaller than crows to the 47-foot (15-m) long *Giganotosaurus*.

Triassic The first of the three periods of the Mesozoic Era, and of dinosaurs, from 245 million to 200 million years ago.

Vegetation Plant life.

Vertebrates Animals with backbones, including amphibians, birds, fish, mammals and reptiles.

Index